# THE NORTH AMERICAN
# FREE TRADE
# AGREEMENT

❖ ❖ ❖

by George W. Grayson

# HEADLINE SERIES

No. 299　　　　FOREIGN POLICY ASSOCIATION　　　　Summer

# The North American Free Trade Agreement

## by George W. Grayson

Cover Design: Canzani Graphics Communications, Inc.　　　　$5.95

## The Author

GEORGE W. GRAYSON, professor of government at the College of William and Mary, has made 30 research trips to Mexico since 1976, and lectures regularly at the National War College, the Army War College and the Foreign Service Institute of the U.S. Department of State. His writings include *The United States and Mexico: Patterns of Influence* (1984), *Oil and Mexican Foreign Policy* (1988), *The Mexican Labor Machine: Power, Politics, and Patronage* (1989), *Prospects for Democracy in Mexico* (1990) and *The Church in Contemporary Mexico* (1992) as well as numerous articles. Professor Grayson earned his Ph.D. at the Paul H. Nitze School of Advanced International Studies of The Johns Hopkins University and his J.D. at the College of William and Mary. He has served as a member of the state legislature of Virginia for 18 years.

## The Foreign Policy Association

The Foreign Policy Association is a private, nonprofit, nonpartisan educational organization. Its purpose is to stimulate wider interest and more effective participation in, and greater understanding of, world affairs among American citizens. Among its activities is the continuous publication, dating from 1935, of the HEADLINE SERIES. The author is responsible for factual accuracy and for the views expressed. FPA itself takes no position on issues of U.S. foreign policy.

HEADLINE SERIES (ISSN 0017-8780) is published four times a year, Winter, Spring, Summer and Fall, by the Foreign Policy Association, Inc., 729 Seventh Ave., New York, N.Y. 10019. Chairman, Michael H. Coles; President, R.T. Curran; Editor in Chief, Nancy L. Hoepli; Senior Editors, Ann R. Monjo and K.M. Rohan. Subscription rates, $15.00 for 4 issues; $25.00 for 8 issues; $30.00 for 12 issues. Single copy price $5.95. Discount 25% on 10 to 99 copies; 30% on 100 to 499; 35% on 500 to 999; 40% on 1,000 or more. Payment must accompany all orders. Postage and handling: $2.50 for first copy; $.50 each additional copy. Second-class postage paid at New York, N.Y. POSTMASTER: Send address changes to HEADLINE SERIES, Foreign Policy Association, 729 Seventh Ave., New York, N.Y. 10019. Copyright 1993 by Foreign Policy Association, Inc. Design by K.M. Rohan. Printed at Science Press, Ephrata, Pennsylvania. Summer 1992. Published April 1993.

Library of Congress Catalog Card No. 93-070279
ISBN 0-87124-151-X

# FOREWORD

The intensifying debate within the United States over the pros and cons of the proposed North American Free Trade Agreement is really a debate over the wisdom of opening our southern border to the free flow of goods and services between the United States and Mexico. This is understandable. A free-trade agreement between the United States and Canada already exists and is in its fifth year. To many Americans, it seems logical to have such an arrangement with a country that shares our culture, language and level of development. This is not the case with Mexico, a developing country of 88 million people who speak Spanish, have a very different culture and enjoy a considerably lower standard of living than that of the United States.

It should come as no surprise, therefore, that the proposed free-trade agreement has generated strong fears within the United States regarding its ability to compete with a country whose workers earn about one-tenth the wages of U.S. workers and whose enforcement of labor and environmental standards in particular has traditionally been less stringent. The fact that the U.S. economy has been in recession during most of the debate over free trade with Mexico has exacerbated these concerns.

Perhaps paradoxically, however, the proposed free-trade agreement has also led others to argue that free trade with Mexico will produce increased trade and investment in the United States, leading to new jobs and a more internationally competitive U.S. economy. The vision is of a "win-win" situation, in which both Mexico and the United States stand to gain from the accelerated removal of the remaining barriers to free trade between our two countries.

Who is right and who is wrong? What will free trade really

mean for the United States and for specific groups of individual Americans? In order to help clarify the stakes involved in such an important policy issue, which is simultaneously a domestic and a foreign policy issue, a delegation from the Board of Governors of the Foreign Policy Association made a fact-finding visit to Mexico in October 1991. During their visit, in which I participated as an adviser, they met with President Carlos Salinas de Gortari and Mrs. Salinas, Foreign Secretary Fernando Solana Morales, Secretary of Commerce and Industrial Development Jaime Serra Puche, Secretary of Programming and Budget Ernesto Zedillo Ponce de León, Secretary of Finance and Public Credit Pedro Aspe Armella, the leaders of the two main opposition parties, Cuauhtémoc Cárdenas of the Party of the Democratic Revolution and Luis H. Alvarez of the National Action party (PAN), economists, businessmen and other private citizens.

The Mexico trip confirmed the Foreign Policy Association's conviction that it was important for U.S. citizens to be better informed about the North American free-trade issue so as to participate more effectively in the often confusing debate on the agreement. The association therefore asked George W. Grayson, a leading U.S. expert on Mexico, U.S.-Mexican relations and the politics of North American free trade to write this HEADLINE SERIES.

As the controversy generated over the proposed creation of a North American free-trade area continues to produce new publications, Dr. Grayson's contribution is noteworthy for the breadth of its focus and its accessibility to readers who are neither experts on Mexico nor on the proposed North American Free Trade Agreement. It should allow individual citizens to decide for themselves whether North American free trade is good or bad for them and for their country.

*Susan Kaufman Purcell*
*Americas Society*
*New York City*

# Introduction: Salinas

In early 1991 some 100 self-described witches gathered in Mexico City to brood over black magic, exotic hexes, tarot cards, and other trappings of the occult. These otherworldly spiritualists even found time to discuss the proposed North American Free Trade Agreement (Nafta) between Mexico, Canada and the United States. This initiative would eliminate impediments to commerce to take advantage of Canada's natural resources, U.S. capital and know-how, and Mexico's cheap, abundant labor. It would create a free-trade zone composed of 370 million consumers who each year produce more than $6.5 trillion in goods and services. Antonio Vázquez, the leading warlock, spoke for his colleagues when he said: "Free trade will be good for...[Mexico's] economy, but not for our culture." Although the sorcerers backed Nafta in a statement to the press, they resolved to protect their traditions and customs from an anticipated cultural invasion from north of the Rio Grande.

In many ways, Vázquez and his colleagues articulated the

ambivalence that many Mexicans and Canadians feel toward linking their economies more closely with a neighboring superpower. On the one hand, they realized that free-trade zones typically spur commercial activity, attract investment, promote growth and create employment. On the other hand, they feared that, like proverbial mice in bed with an elephant—a metaphor first employed by former Canadian Prime Minister Pierre Elliott Trudeau (1968–79; 1980–84)— the national identities of Mexico and Canada might be attenuated by a tidal wave of McDonald's restaurants, CNN broadcasts, NIKE tennis shoes and Hershey chocolate bars.

Controversy was nothing new to Mexico's President Carlos Salinas de Gortari (1988– ), who—along with U.S. President George Bush (1989–93)—was the prime mover behind Nafta. Salinas had shattered one taboo after another upon taking office on December 1, 1988. He ousted "untouchable" labor barons, sold the state-owned airline, telephone company and steel mills, slashed tax rates and threw tax cheats behind bars, and reprivatized the banking system. He also launched a reform of sacrosanct communal farms *(ejidos)*, invited a Texas oil firm with an all-foreign crew to drill in Campeche Sound, and reorganized Petróleos Mexicanos (Pemex), the state oil monopoly. Furthermore, he normalized relations with the Roman Catholic Church, long reviled as part of the exploitative, prerevolutionary social order by intellectuals, union leaders, leftist politicians and activists in his own Institutional Revolutionary party (PRI). With the fall of the Communist party in the former U.S.S.R., the PRI, founded in 1929, has governed longer than any other political party in the world.

In contrast to Soviet communism's last leader, Mikhail Gorbachev (1985–91), who simultaneously promoted *glasnost* (openness) and *perestroika* (restructuring the economy), Salinas stressed economic liberalization over a political opening. He did this to avoid generating demands that could not be satisfied before Mexico had achieved robust, sustained growth. Nonetheless, he recognized the victo-

## Canada, United States and Mexico: Selected Economic Indicators

| Country | Population (millions) | GDP per capita (dollars) | Imports from the United States (billions) | Exports to the United States (billions) |
|---|---|---|---|---|
| Canada | 27 | $ 20,804 | $ 85.1 | $ 91.1 |
| United States | 256 | 22,183 | | |
| Mexico | 88 | 3,283 | 33.3 | 31.1 |

Source: 1992 Facts on File

Robert Mansfield

ries of opposition gubernatorial candidates over his own party's standard-bearers for the first time in 60 years. He also scheduled new state elections in Guanajuato and San Luis Potosí when losing nominees of the center-right National Action party (PAN) alleged fraud in August 1991. Later, he accepted the "resignation" of the newly inaugurated PRI governor of Michoacán when the nationalist-leftist Democratic Revolutionary party (PRD) staged aggressive demonstrations to protest his mid-1992 victory. Another mark of pluralism is the 4,000 elected municipal offices (of 19,000 nationwide) held by the PAN, the PRD and other opposition groups. In addition, Mexico's *jefe máximo* diminished the influence of the labor and peasant sectors in a reform of his own Tammany Hall-style PRI. Finally, he lavished several billion dollars a year on a National Solidarity Program (Pronasol) designed to involve peasants and shantytown dwellers in development projects that they, not self-serving party bosses, identified as crucial to their communities. Indeed, if a local Rip van Winkle had awakened in the early 1990s after a generation of slumber, he would have rubbed his eyes in disbelief at the changes besetting his once hugely bureaucratized, statist, corrupt country.

He would have been even more awestruck by Salinas's

most dramatic innovation: a new relationship with the United States embodied in Nafta. Fundamental to Mexico's diplomacy was the president's belief that continental interdependence would catapult his country from the nineteenth to the twentieth century. Unlike many largely symbolic programs proclaimed by his predecessors—the New International Economic Order, the Charter of Economic Rights and Duties of States, the World Energy Plan and the International Meeting for Cooperation and Development, for example—Salinas's commitment to economic liberalization represented real, not just rhetorical, change.

## Salinas in Office

Salinas, as planning and budget secretary in President Miguel de la Madrid Hurtado's administration (1982–88), spearheaded the dismantling of Mexico's import-substitution approach to industrialization (instead of importing finished goods from abroad, Mexico manufactured its own products for domestic consumption). That model had impelled the country's "economic miracle" of the post-World War II period. Yet, by the mid-1970s the spry, eager infant industries of the previous generation had grown porcine, lethargic, inefficient and whiny. Sheltered by import permits and formidable tariffs, many of these firms produced expensive goods of inferior quality that were uncompetitive in foreign markets. Worse still, import-substitution spawned a huge bureaucracy infamous for featherbedding, incompetence, delays and surly officials who demanded under-the-table *mordida* payments to furnish documents and services.

De la Madrid and Salinas realized that Mexico had to break out of its protectionist cocoon to boost labor productivity, activate the domestic business community, promote exports, stimulate investment, obtain foreign loans and attract state-of-the-art technology. As a first step toward integrating his nation into the international economic system, de la Madrid signed a Bilateral Subsidies Understanding with the United States in 1985. This accord stipulated that his country would phase out export subsidies in exchange for an injury test in countervailing-duty* litigation. In other words, U.S. producers of, say, steel would have to demonstrate actual harm suffered from Mexican steel exports that benefited from unfair trade practices before penalties could be imposed on these goods. To build on this important foundation, the two nations entered into a Bilateral Trade and Investment Framework Agreement in November 1987. Although appearing more symbolic than substantive, this pact created a consultative mechanism for resolving disputes in two often nettlesome areas—trade and investment. Two years later, the United States and Mexico took advantage of the work begun earlier and reached a second trade and investment understanding. In 1986, moreover, de la Madrid and Salinas championed their country's membership in the General Agreement on Tariffs and Trade (GATT).* GATT is a 108-member organization devoted to promoting trade through eradicating barriers and conferring reciprocal benefits on member nations. In June of that year, de la Madrid also dropped his threat to join a debtors' cartel to confront the United States over Mexico's $100-billion debt owed to private and public lenders. This action proved a critical juncture in bilateral relations.

As chief executive, Salinas removed obstacles to trade and welcomed imports as part of a strategy to force domestic corporations to compete with their foreign counterparts. After all, in the words of *The Economist* (London), "Mexico's private sector is still dominated by a tight oligarchy, where connections matter more than merit and where the ruling patriarchs are reluctant to give up control." "Our first challenge was privatizing the [so-called] private sector," stated Pedro Aspe Armella, the country's finance secretary (and a leading contender to become Mexico's next president). In the process, Mexico dropped its top tariffs from 100 percent to 20 percent and jettisoned licensing requirements for 95 percent of the nation's goods purchased abroad. In the six years after joining GATT, Mexico achieved as much trade liberal-

*All starred words appear in glossary on page 77.

ization as the United States attained in the 40 years after reaching its protectionist zenith in 1930.

## Closer U.S.-Mexican Relations

Even though the youthful president had yet to present a blueprint for linking his country with the global economy, his enthusiasm for market principles and readiness to pay interest on his nation's mammoth international debt earned him trust and respect abroad. Salinas's Mexico had the distinction of becoming the first beneficiary of the 1989 Brady Plan for reducing Latin America's commercial bank debts. Under this initiative, named for U.S. Treasury Secretary Nicholas F. Brady, the banks offered Mexico one or a blend of three options: a 35 percent reduction on the principal of loans, a corresponding cut in interest rates to 6.25 percent, or refinancing amounting to 60 percent of annual interest charges. This was the first time since the debt crisis had erupted in the early 1980s that the United States had proposed reduced interest rates for greatly overborrowed countries.

Lest it chill ever-warmer economic and diplomatic relations with its northern neighbor, Salinas's condemnation of the December 1989 U.S. invasion of Panama was one of the mildest in the region, even though the action contravened Mexico's cherished principles of nonintervention, respect for sovereignty, and peaceful settlement of disputes.

As fervently as he desired a trade accord, Salinas did not become a toady of the United States. For example, he excoriated the abduction from Guadalajara and trial in Los Angeles of Humberto Alvarez Macháin, a physician who allegedly participated in the torture and murder of a U.S. Drug Enforcement Administration agent in 1985. Meanwhile, Mexico continued to demonstrate its independence at the United Nations, albeit in a low-keyed style. In 1992 it voted with the United States only 20 percent of the time compared to a 60 percent U.S.-Canadian coincidence. Mexican diplomats, however, generally refrained from strident criticism of their neighbor and, on issues deemed "important" by the U.S. De-

Reuters/Bettmann

**Mexican, U.S. and Canadian trade ministers initialed Nafta
October 7, 1992, with their leaders, Carlos Salinas, George Bush
and Brian Mulroney, witnessing the ceremony.**

partment of State, cast half of their votes with the United States (the comparable Canadian figure was 75 percent).

For his part, President Bush, who developed a cordial rapport with Salinas during eight bilateral meetings, also made a concerted effort in public statements to accentuate economic positives while downplaying political negatives. Thus, he handled discreetly such acutely sensitive questions as drug trafficking, human-rights violations and electoral chicanery—activities whose open condemnation had embittered U.S.-Mexican relations during the Reagan era (1981–89).

## Move Toward a Free-Trade Agreement

Salinas's bold attempt to integrate Mexico's economy with that of the United States began in earnest after he failed to broaden Mexico's commercial and financial ties with Japan and Western Europe. In early 1990, Salinas spent 10 days in Western Europe where he met with the leaders of Britain, West Germany, Belgium, Switzerland and Portugal. Although then Prime Minister Margaret Thatcher encouraged his efforts, the other hosts graciously conveyed a disheartening message: "We admire your market-oriented strategy to open and modernize Mexico's hidebound economy, but East Europe will be the target of our capital investment, finance and commercial activities."

This polite rebuff reinforced Salinas's belief that Mexico must find another dynamic partner to avoid becoming a stagnant backwater as trading blocs emerged in Western Europe, in the Pacific Rim, and between Canada and the United States. The United States was an obvious choice. Location, tradition and a spiderweb of economic ties pointed Salinas northward. Also impressive was the success of the 1988 U.S.-Canada Free Trade Agreement (CFTA) in stimulating bilateral trade and attracting investor attention to Canada. The bonds between Mexico and the United States were already noteworthy, as evidenced by the 1989 flow of exports ($25 billion), investment ($5.5 billion), and traveler expenditures ($5.7 billion) from the United States to its southern neighbor. For their part, Mexican consumers purchased U.S. goods and services valued at $27.2 billion, making Mexico the third-largest export market for the United States in 1989. Almost 2,000 *maquiladoras,* Spanish for border assembly plants, employing a half-million Mexicans, fortified the bilateral linkage, as did the growing interrelationship between the New York and Mexico City stock exchanges.

Other signs of mounting United States-Mexican interdependence included increased migration, tourism, telephone calls, telegraph messages and media contacts.

In addition, Pemex had furnished 44 percent of the almost 600 million barrels of oil stored in the U.S. Strategic Petroleum Reserve. And Pemex and private Mexican firms purchased upward of $100 million worth of oil equipment and services from U.S. suppliers in 1989.

## Pact Gains Support

In May 1990 Salinas endorsed a free-trade agreement with the United States, a concept that he had opposed immediately after his inauguration. Just a few years earlier, the issue had been a political "third rail." Even publicly favoring such a scheme would have ended the career of most politicians in defensively nationalistic Mexico, where the "colossus of the north" is frequently blamed for all kinds of real and imagined evils—in large measure because the United States violently seized half of Mexico's territory in the mid-nineteenth century. An example of this near-paranoid defensiveness surfaced in mid-1980 when Mexican officials and newspapers had a field day accusing Washington of stealing rain by diverting hurricanes from Mexico's shores. The villain was the U.S. National Oceanic and Atmospheric Administration, whose hurricane-hunter aircraft had allegedly intercepted a storm named "Ignacio" off Mexico's Pacific coast in October 1979, thereby contributing to the country's worst drought in 20 years. Mexican observers, including the director of the country's National Meteorological Service, apparently believed that Yankee ingenuity was so great that Uncle Sam could bend Mother Nature to his indomitable will.

Reactive nationalism aside, Salinas committed himself to economic integration. Mexico's highly centralized political system, buttressed by ubiquitous official influence in the media, guaranteed broad acceptance of the presidential initiative. Taking their cue from the Los Pinos presidential palace, most PRI leaders applauded a free-trade pact; the 64-member Mexican Senate overwhelmingly embraced the proposal; many editorial writers wrote glowingly of the venture; major business associations backed an accord; and the Confederation of Mexican Workers, the 5.5 million-member trade union federation that forms part of the PRI's corporatist structure, grudgingly recommended a bilateral economic agreement.

# The Fast-Track Showdown

On September 21, 1990, following six months of unofficial, exploratory discussions, Salinas formally told President Bush that he wanted to begin talks on Nafta. Earlier, the U.S. bureaucracy had been divided over the priority for forging such a pact. From the outset, the National Security Council (NSC), along with the departments of Commerce, State and Treasury, welcomed the idea of a free-trade agreement and urged full speed ahead on the proposal. Initially, the Office of the U.S. Trade Representative (USTR), the nation's pivotal agency in trade matters, and the Department of Agriculture both expressed caution about the venture. USTR, in particular, knew from its protracted efforts on the U.S.-Canada Free Trade Agreement in the late 1980s how much groundwork had to be laid with Congress and the private sector before negotiations could prosper. USTR head Carla A. Hills was also concerned that embarking on Nafta would delay completion of the Uruguay Round,* the eighth set of multilateral trade talks under

The above has benefited greatly, especially with respect to pithy quotations gathered by the authors, from Alan F. Holmer and Judith H. Bello, "The Fast Track Debate: A Prescription for Pragmatism," *The International Lawyer* 26, No. 1 (Spring 1992), pp. 183–99.

GATT. (After all, Mexico purchased less than 5 percent of U.S. goods and services shipped abroad, while the other GATT members accounted for nearly 100 percent.) By September, however, USTR was convinced that Nafta would complement, not conflict with, efforts to conclude GATT talks.

The Uruguay Round, which has involved contentious, multilateral negotiations, commenced in the Uruguayan resort city of Punta del Este in 1986. These parleys have transcended the traditional GATT agenda concerning manufactured goods in order to address obstructions to trade in financial services and agricultural items, as well as protecting patents, trademarks, copyrights, computer software and other intellectual property. A conflict over price supports and export subsidies between the 12-member integrated European Community (EC) and a U.S.-led coalition of agricultural exporters paralyzed the global talks, thereby giving greater impetus to Nafta. To diversify his trade options, Bush officially notified Congress on September 25, 1990, that he intended to negotiate a free-trade pact with Mexico. Subsequently, he requested a two-year extension of "fast-track"* authority to provide more time for Congress to consider any agreement that might emerge from the Uruguay Round and to accommodate any free-trade accord that might be signed with Mexico.

### Fast-Track Defined

What is fast-track? How does it affect trade legislation? The musings of some humorists aside, it is neither a speedy race-course, a zany dance step nor a high-speed sports event. Rather, fast-track reflects the American genius for hammering out compromises. The U.S. Constitution empowers the President to conduct foreign affairs, including entering into trade agreements; Congress is vested with authority "to regulate commerce with foreign nations." Yet lawmakers found out in 1930 that trying to write tariff legislation could boomerang. In that year, the House and Senate passed the infamous Hawley-Smoot Tariff Act to protect Depression-injured industries through sharply higher levies on imports. What architects of this statute failed to anticipate was the swift retaliation that Hawley-Smoot provoked from trading partners. The upshot was a downward spiral in both world commerce and the U.S. economy.

How, then, could the executive branch be permitted the necessary leeway and credibility to negotiate intricate trade arrangements without unsympathetic legislators disfiguring its handiwork through a barrage of amendments that often delay and cripple controversial bills? The answer turned out to be fast-track. This mechanism empowers presidential representatives to forge a trade deal with one or more foreign governments. Congress must then accept or reject the accord as a package; no changes are allowed.

This concept, embedded in the Trade Act of 1974, established an executive-legislative partnership in trade affairs. The Omnibus Trade and Competitiveness Act of 1988 further stated that fast-track authority could be extended for two years if the president so requested, provided, of course, that neither a key committee (Ways and Means in the House; Finance in the Senate) nor either legislative chamber passed a disallowing resolution within 90 days of the White House request. Absent congressional disapproval, fast-track procedural protection would apply to any trade agreement submitted 90 calendar days before the expiration of the expedited authority. In the case of Nafta, the deadline for submitting the pact was 90 days before May 31, 1993. The signed agreement was submitted on December 17, 1992.

In summary, fast-track allows expedited trade negotiations to take place under the following formal and informal procedures:

• The President provides at least 60 days' notice to the House Ways and Means and Senate Finance committees of his intention to commence trade negotiations with a foreign country;

• The President informs the House of Representatives and

the Senate of his readiness to enter into an agreement at least 90 calendar days before he signs the accord;

• After signing the pact, the President submits to the House and the Senate the agreement, an implementing bill crafted in concert with congressional leaders, a statement of administrative action proposed to implement the accord, and detailed supporting information that embraces an explanation of how the agreement achieves U.S. negotiating objectives;

• Provided the executive branch has met all procedural hurdles, the House (45 days in committees; 15 days on the floor) and the Senate (15 days in committees; 15 days on the floor) may take up to 90 legislative days to consider the legislation. Speech-making in each chamber is limited to 20 hours. Debate time in the House is split equally between proponents and opponents; in the Senate, the time is divided between the majority and minority leaders;

• Then each house separately—by a majority—votes aye or nay on the unamendable legislative package, which cannot be filibustered in the Senate.

## *The Case for Fast-Track*

In 1991 proponents reiterated several arguments in favor of fast-track. First, the mechanism ensures that the initiative for trade negotiations lies with the executive branch, while conferring upon Congress ultimate control over an agreement's fate. To deprive the President of this authority would discourage him from involving legislators in the negotiating process. Second, a vote for fast-track endorsed process not substance. Members could reject an agreement considered harmful to the nation or to their constituents. Third, extending fast-track was crucial to continued U.S. efforts to reduce trade barriers in a world where protectionism was alive and well. Fourth, the process helped the United States conclude free-trade agreements with Israel (1985) and Canada. Finally, foreign countries would deem it futile to bargain with the United States if any agreement were subject to being overturned or adorned with "Christmas-tree amendments" in Congress in order to protect powerful U.S. industries.

With respect to this last matter, Representative Sam M. Gibbons (D-Fla.), a free-trader and chairman of the subcommittee on trade of the Committee on Ways and Means, pointed out that Congress conceived of fast-track after defeating two agreements negotiated under GATT's Kennedy Round (1964–67). The reaction of U.S. trading partners was, he said: "Listen, unless you reform your congressional procedures, we aren't dealing with you anymore. You are not a reliable bargainer."

Opponents of Nafta got their licks in against fast-track. First, they insisted that, while appropriate for negotiations among GATT members, accelerated approval authority was not intended for talks with just a country or two. Second, they claimed the Mexicans were so eager for Nafta that, in the words of Senator Howard M. Metzenbaum (D-Ohio), they "will continue to negotiate with or without the fast-track." Third, critics contended that the Reagan Administration had failed to consult Congress sufficiently on the U.S.-Canada Free Trade Agreement, and that Bush's representatives would engage only in *pro forma* contacts with the legislative branch. "In my experience, the [Bush-Congress] consultations have not been meaningful," said Senator Thomas A. Daschle (D-S. Dak.). "Muggers meet directly with their victims, too, but we don't call it consultations." Although some detractors admitted that Bush's team might truly consult with the Ways and Means and Finance committees, they argued that rank-and-file legislators who belonged to neither panel would be frozen out of the loop. Deprived of the chance to offer floor amendments, such members would have little or no influence on the trade talks. Fourth, a few members viewed fast-track as an unconstitutional abridgment of the checks-and-balances system, while others, who conceded its legality, berated the process as an "abdication," "abrogation," or "surrender" of legislative prerogatives. They inveighed against giving the White House *"carte blanche,"* a "blank check," or "keys to the store."

A final argument against the special negotiating authority touched on the merits of the pact itself. An amalgam of labor, environmental, consumer and religious organizations submitted that fast-track would facilitate a fundamentally flawed agreement. Nafta, they argued, would eliminate American jobs as factories migrated across the border to take advantage of sweat-shop conditions amid lax environmental rules and human-rights abuses. For example, Mike Clark, former president of Friends of the Earth, said that "the fast-track is a slippery track, a wrong track and it should be stopped dead in its tracks." In a similar vein, the Reverend Pharis Harvey, executive director of the International Labor Rights Education & Research Fund, compared a free-trade accord with Mexico to a "shotgun wedding" that could well lead to a "lose-lose" situation for both countries. Added Harvey, "The Administration is giving us a blueprint for a train wreck."

Critics of fast-track took advantage of a prolonged recession and high unemployment in the United States, Nafta foe Harris Wofford's Democratic upset victory in a special U.S. Senate race in Pennsylvania, and White House preoccupation with Operation Desert Shield/Desert Storm to press their case with Congress. At the same time that United Nations forces were routing Iraqi President Saddam Hussein's troops from Kuwait in February 1991, the anti-fast-track coalition was attempting to vanquish Nafta through lobbying on Capitol Hill.

## Bush Enters the Fray

Nearly two months after Iraq's defeat in March 1991, President Bush began his counterattack against Nafta foes. In this battle, he enjoyed enthusiastic backing from the Coalition for Trade Expansion, which constituted a veritable "Who's Who" of major corporations (most of the same firms now belong to the USA-Nafta Coalition). The chief executive and his business allies argued that since 1986 U.S. exports to Mexico had doubled to $28.4 billion, creating 315,000 export-related jobs in the United States, and that Nafta would generate 113,000 new trade-focused jobs in

Texas alone. "If Americans are honestly concerned about the environment, the standard of living in Mexico and about democratization," averred MIT Professor Rudiger Dornbusch, "they cannot escape the recognition that a thriving, open-market economy will raise living standards, foster individual freedom, decentralize political power and allow people to organize around local issues."

Prospects brightened for fast-track approval after Bush, fearful of a setback, announced an "Action Plan" keyed to the concerns of labor and environmental groups. Central to this plan was a memorandum of understanding on worker health and safety signed by U.S. Labor Secretary Lynn M. Martin and her Mexican counterpart. This document provided for the exchange of information not only on worker health and safety, but also working conditions, labor-standards enforcement, resolution of labor-management disputes, collective-bargaining agreements, social security, credit institutions, labor statistics, labor quality and productivity. Nafta would make it possible, Secretary Martin said, "to move earnestly with our neighbors to the south to address child labor and safety and health concerns and improve the lives of our working men and women."

In addition, the self-styled environmental president assured Congress of his commitment to:
• Strict health and safety standards for agricultural imports to prevent Mexican products that do not meet U.S. health or safety requirements from entering the United States;
• Transition periods of more than 10 years for reducing U.S. tariffs in certain sectors and industries;
• Worker-adjustment programs for workers who may lose their jobs as a result of an agreement with Mexico; and
• Exclusion of labor mobility and immigration laws from the negotiations.

At the direction of Bush and Salinas, environmental authorities in both countries devised an Integrated Environmental Plan for the Border. Following 17 public hearings, the United States committed substantial resources ($384 million in 1992–93) as did Mexico ($460 million in 1992–94) to implement the first phase of this program. Their highest priority was wastewater-treatment projects for twin cities along the border (San Diego/Tijuana, Imperial Valley/Mexicali, Nogales/Nogales and Laredo/Nuevo Laredo—see map, page 25). Monies were also promised for enforcement, environmental health, emergency planning and response, and the monitoring and mitigation of transboundary air pollution. This initiative was designed to blunt the charge that Mexico would remain a "pollution haven" for unscrupulous foreign firms if Nafta were approved. In March 1991 Salinas aggressively raised his ecological profile by closing the aged, sulfur-belching Azcapotzalco oil refinery in Mexico City, which employed more than 5,000 workers.

### Environmental Crackdown on Border Businesses

Between 1989 and 1991, the environmental and natural resources budget for Mexico's Ministry of Ecology and Urban Development (Sedue)—succeeded in 1992 by the Ministry of Social Development (Sedesol)—shot up from $6 million to $36 million, and the agency closed 28 border businesses for environmental infractions in 1991. Sedesol's team of 200 inspectors ensured, among other things, that the amount of hazardous waste from maquiladoras that was disposed of properly doubled from 14.5 percent in 1990 to 31 percent a year later. Overall, Mexico devoted $1.8 billion of its 1991 budget to the environment—the equivalent of 0.7 percent of the country's gross domestic product (GDP).

Bush and Salinas's attentiveness to ecological issues helped to split the labor-environmental axis aligned against free-trade negotiations. With the promise that ecological organizations would be represented on panels advising U.S. Trade Representative Hills, the National Wildlife Federation and the National Audubon Society expressed cautious support for fast-track. In a *New York Times* column, National Wildlife Federation President Jay D. Hair illuminated the progress made by ecologists:

When a handful of environmental groups first stepped into the free-trade discussion, they were greeted with condescending incredulousness by financial experts who viewed the talks as belonging to a closed club devoted exclusively to commercial considerations. That presumption—that environmentalism and economics don't mix—has been punctured.

Enhancing the prospect for fast-track authorization was the resolute backing that Nafta enjoyed from key U.S. policymakers, many of whom were Texans. In addition to President Bush, fellow Texans Secretary of State James A. Baker 3d, Commerce Secretary Robert A. Mosbacher, Senate Finance Committee chairman Lloyd Bentsen (D-Tex.), Senator Phil Gramm (R-Tex.) and Representative Bill Archer (R-Tex.), ranking minority member of the Committee on Ways and Means, knew firsthand Mexico's crucial importance to the United States. House Speaker Thomas S. Foley (D-Wash.), House Majority Leader Richard A. Gephardt (D-Mo.), and House Committee on Ways and Means Chairman Dan Rostenkowski (D-Ill.) also cast their lot with fast-track. Gephardt, on whom organized labor had counted to defeat fast-track, made clear that his support for accelerated negotiating authority did not commit him to vote for a Nafta that failed to address labor and environmental concerns. Of his intended vigilance, the majority leader warned: "I am serving notice today that Congress will...[keep the pressure on] Chairman Rostenkowski [and] Senator Bentsen and I will sound like the song by the [P]olice that goes, 'Every breath you take, every step you take, every move you make, we'll be watching you.' Trust but verify: that will be our policy."

Ultimately, the President succeeded in elevating fast-track approval to a referendum on protectionism. "Having already opposed [the extremely popular] Bush on the use of force in Iraq," wrote David S. Cloud of the *Congressional Quarterly,* "many Democrats fear[ed] a vote that would be portrayed as economic isolationism." In mid-May 1991, Congress killed resolutions to reject fast-track authority. On May 23, 1991,

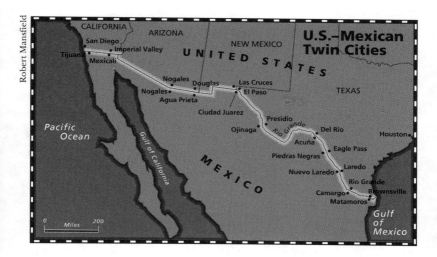

Robert Mansfield

U.S.–Mexican Twin Cities

the House of Representatives voted 231 to 192 against a resolution sponsored by Representative Byron L. Dorgan (D-
N.Dak.) to deny fast-track authority; the next day the Senate
turned thumbs down, by a 59 to 36 vote, on a similar disallowing measure proposed by Senator Ernest F. Hollings (D-
S.C.). The overwhelming majority of opponents to fast-track
extension in both houses were Democrats (170 of the 192
noes in the House; 31 of 36 noes in the Senate). These votes
followed repudiation of anti-fast-track initiatives by the
House Committee on Ways and Means (27 to 9) and the
Senate Finance Committee (15 to 3)—bodies that have principal jurisdiction over trade legislation.

In the main, fast-track opponents represented states with
smokestack industries and strong unions (the Northeast and
the "rust belt"), major textile sectors (the Carolinas), and
large agricultural subsidies (the Dakotas). Most supporters
came from the border, the Sun Belt and coastal states, or
were just philosophically congenial to free trade. Six of ten
members of the Hispanic Caucus backed fast-track, while
only 3 of the 24-member congressional Black Caucus supported the initiative. Of 28 congresswomen, 18 endorsed the

extension of fast-track, 9 opposed it, and 1, Barbara F. Vucanovich (R-Nev.), voiced opposition but did not vote.

Nafta benefited from the fact that a two-year extension of fast-track was crucial to completing the Uruguay Round. Many legislators who expressed qualms about a North American pact were reluctant to capsize global negotiations that had been churning along for five years.

Further evidence that the fast-track outcome was no harbinger of the ultimate Nafta vote came in House Resolution 146 sponsored by Gephardt, who wanted to propitiate the AFL-CIO (union members picketed him during a visit to his St. Louis district following the fast-track vote). This nonbinding legislation expressed the "sense of the House" that the Congress could suspend the accelerated negotiating authority if the Administration failed to keep its May 1 commitment to environmental safeguards, employee safety and worker-adjustment assistance. HR 146 not only put Bush on notice that Congress would hold his feet to the fire, but also provided cover for legislators concerned about offending trade unionists. "There are members on both sides of the aisle who want to vote for something satisfying, as much as they can, labor's demands," commented Rostenkowski. Initially, Bush feared that the resolution would offend Mexico and resented being, in the words of the Ways and Means chairman, "nickled and dimed." In the view of the *Congressional Quarterly,* the President wound up supporting the measure in hopes that it would attract more votes to fast-track extension and bolster the U.S. position in the troubled GATT talks in Geneva. The upshot of the executive-legislative politicking was to extend fast-track for Nafta and the Uruguay Round, provided the White House submitted the texts of these deals to Congress by May 31, 1993. Ultimately, this deadline posed no barrier to the continental accord. In early 1993, however, the Clinton Administration made it known that it would seek a further extension of fast-track power for the delay-bedeviled Uruguay Round.

# The Negotiations

Once the fast-track prerogative was secure, negotiations began in mid-1991—with responsibility for their conduct vested in the U.S. Trade Representative. The Trade Expansion Act of 1962 created the Special Representative for Trade Negotiations, predecessor to the USTR, as an executive branch agency that was obligated to report to Congress. Thus the legislation removed prime responsibility for trade matters from the State Department, which, allegedly, stressed broad foreign policy goals over trade, was too sensitive to the interests of foreign governments, and had become a "fudge factory" that was slow to reach decisions. Nor, it was argued, could the Commerce Department, with its powerful business constituency, bring a national perspective to trade policy. Compared to the somnambulant, hidebound Commerce Department, which has some 31,000 employees spread around the world, the USTR is a dynamic, take-charge agency with some 160 officials. "No one ever retires from USTR," averred an alumnus of the trade agency. "They are men and women with 'Type A' personalities who work their behinds off for 10 years or so and then move elsewhere in the federal government or get rich lobbying."

The struggle over fast-track had strengthened the bonds between USTR's Hills and her Mexican counterpart, Jaime Serra Puche, head of the Ministry of Commerce and Industrial Development (Secofi). The process was complicated only slightly by Canada's late-1990 request for inclusion in discussions for an accord that would form the world's largest free-trade zone, stretching from the Yukon to the Yucatán. Both the United States and Mexico were apprehensive lest Canadian involvement slow or hobble negotiations that would have the biggest payoff for their two countries. Canada pledged to withdraw from the talks if it constituted an impediment to their successful conclusion; similarly, the Bush and Salinas administrations reserved the right to excuse Canada if its presence proved an obstacle. In fact, Canada's participation assuaged some Mexican fears that their country, with 1/20 the GDP of the United States, would be overwhelmed if it entered the proposed trade configuration alone with an economic behemoth.

### The Talks Begin

On June 12, 1991, the trade ministers launched the talks in Toronto at what became the first of seven Trilateral Ministerial Oversight meetings, involving Hills, Serra Puche and Canadian International Trade Minister Michael H. Wilson. The main bureaucratic players in Washington shared the same interests, although there was a slight difference of emphasis among the agencies. USTR viewed the pact as a means to lock in the market-focused reforms accomplished by the de la Madrid and Salinas regimes. The Treasury Department also wished to institutionalize Mexico's version of perestroika, while expanding opportunities below the Rio Grande for U.S. financial institutions and other investors. The Commerce Department sought greater access for U.S. exports to Mexico. The Agriculture Department wanted to eliminate burdensome licensing requirements confronting grains and other farm exports. The Transportation Department championed access for U.S. truck, rail and bus lines into Mexico's interior. And perceiving relations from a geopolitical vantage point, the State Department and the National Security Council insisted that Nafta meant investment, growth, job-creation and—above all—stability in a neighbor with which the United States shares a 2,000-mile border.

President Salinas also regarded Nafta as giving momentum to sustained development to vault his country from Third World status to First World rank. Not only would increased continental trade attract North American investment, but it would also draw capital from elsewhere in Latin America, Europe and Asia, where entrepreneurs coveted opportunities presented by a secure, expanding market that included the United States. In addition, dismantling protectionism would force Mexico's business community to increase efficiency or risk bankruptcy. And just as the Americans saw Nafta as institutionalizing Mexico's market opening, Salinas regarded the accord as a means to protect his country against any future U.S. return to protectionism.

Canada, which was still assimilating the U.S.-Canada Free Trade Agreement that had sparked a heated internal controversy, pursued largely defensive objectives at the outset of the Nafta negotiations. It did not want Mexico to achieve benefits in the U.S. market that Canada did not enjoy. As one Canadian official expressed it: "We don't want to compromise the preferences that we bought and paid for through tough concessions made in CFTA." Moreover, Canada did not wish the United States to enmesh itself in a series of hub-and-spoke commercial arrangements. In such a configuration, Washington would enjoy preferential access for its exports to spoke nations (Mexico and, possibly, other Latin American states), which—in turn—might not have similar entrée into the markets of other spoke countries. On a positive note, Canada's trade with Mexico had begun to grow, albeit slowly, and it wanted the same opportunities in the Mexican market that U.S. traders enjoyed. Canada also realized from its CFTA experience that negotiating a free-trade agreement thrusts participants into the international limelight. Such attention may lure investors to the countries involved.

## The Negotiators

The Nafta talks focused on six issue categories that were covered by 19 working groups: (1) market access that embraces tariffs, rules of origin, government procurement and related topics; (2) trade rules; (3) services; (4) investment; (5) intellectual-property rights; and (6) dispute settlement. To facilitate harmonious bargaining, the Mexican government removed migration from its negotiating list, while Washington agreed to refrain from pressuring Mexico to modify its constitution's Article 27, which reserves to the state the ownership, exploration and development of petroleum. Early in the talks, Mexico underlined the sensitivity of energy matters when Serra Puche articulated the "five noes" to which its negotiators zealously adhered. They said no to diminishing Mexico's control over the exploration, development, refining and processing of hydrocarbons and primary petrochemicals; to guaranteeing the oil supplies to another country; to relinquishing its monopoly over the commerce, transport, storage and distribution of energy; to permitting risk-contracts in exploration; and to permitting foreign-owned gasoline stations.

USTR designated the "lead agency" for each working group. Even though USTR assumed a lion's share of the leads (seven), it assigned a dozen leads to agencies with functional responsibility for the subject under review. Thus, the Agriculture Department headed the Agriculture Working Group, the Transportation Department led the Land Transportation Working Group, the Treasury Department spearheaded the Financial Working Group, etc. Five considerations explained USTR's meting out of responsibility: (1) its desire to take advantage of agency expertise; (2) its extremely small staff, which was already heavily committed to the Uruguay Round; (3) its previous success with lead-sharing in CFTA; (4) the commitment to collegiality by chief negotiator Julius L. Katz, Hills' second-in-command at USTR; and (5) its belief that involving seven large departments in negotiating Nafta would ensure their support for the final version of the pact. With respect to the last point, USTR's awarding the Commerce Department three leads (automobiles, insurance and trade remedies) helped assuage that agency's initial concerns about Nafta, arising from CFTA, regarding the scope of tariff reductions and the resolution of dumping* and subsidies disputes.

USTR convened a meeting of U.S. leads every two weeks to review progress, harmonize positions, identify opportunities, prepare for upcoming talks, and alert the delegation to "time bombs that might explode." Also participating in these sessions were representatives of the White House domestic policy office and the National Security Council, who frequently expressed impatience over the slow pace of the talks. "I told them," said a ranking USTR official, "that we can complete the agreement tomorrow, but you won't like it and Congress won't pass it."

The U.S. government assigned five or six officials from different agencies to each working group; the Canadians appointed three or four; and the Mexicans, with markedly fewer personnel, generally named several officials at the outset, but added negotiators as the talks progressed and they realized the complexity of the issues. The U.S. and Canadian lead negotiators were in their forties, exhibited negotiating experience thanks to participation in CFTA or GATT, and were usually officials from agencies vested with functional responsibility for their working group's subject matter. At the beginning of negotiations, the United States had five women serving as lead negotiators, and the Canadians had two. In contrast, most Mexican leads were in their thirties; all were male; they boasted little or no previous negotiating experience; and—with three exceptions (agriculture, investment and financial services)—were officials in, or assigned to, the Commerce Ministry. "Bright but inexperienced" was the label that trade insiders initially applied to the Mexicans, many of whom held Oxford, Cambridge or Ivy League degrees. The Mexican government compensated—in part, at least—for its negotiators' anemic background in trade bargaining by hiring as advisers first-rate American and Canadian lawyers, commercial experts and economists. In contrast to the Americans and Canadians, Mexican leads had responsibility for several working groups, with the exception of the Working Group on Energy and Petrochemicals whose lead, Jesús Flores Ayala, had but one assignment. That a half dozen or so men covered 19 working groups fostered coherence within the Mexican team, which kept in continual communication with its superiors and the private sector.

Although variations existed among working groups, the Mexican leads had less bargaining discretion than their U.S. and Canadian counterparts. One explanation for the Mexicans' lack of leeway was the presence at each negotiating site of dozens, sometimes scores, of their business representatives. They often stayed at the same hotel as their country's working groups, with whose leaders they frequently met between bargaining sessions. What accounted for the omnipresence of these private industry "camp followers"? To begin with, the prospect of competition from an economic giant endowed the talks with life-or-death significance for them. In addition, the de la Madrid administration had infuriated its country's entrepreneurs by consulting them little, if at all, before joining GATT. And the academic backgrounds of virtually all Mexican negotiators persuaded the business community of the imperative to acquaint them with the practical consequences of any concessions granted.

As it turned out, Secofi representatives were engaged in several sets of talks: with the United States and Canada; with Pemex and other Mexican agencies that viewed free trade as the political equivalent of fingernails scratching a blackboard; and with Mexican business interests. Although slowing progress in the early months, extensive discussions with Mexico's entrepreneurs throughout the negotiations ensured this influential interest group's support of—or, at least, acquiescence in—the final agreement.

The private sector's intrusiveness, combined with the Mexicans' lack of negotiating experience, helps explain charges that their team leaders occasionally reneged on commitments—a practice that was particularly vexing to Americans in the Government Procurement Working Group. "We got their word on a difficult issue at one meeting, only to see them welsh at the next," according to a participant in the process. For their part, the Mexicans viewed as inconsistent the U.S. government's desire, on the one hand, for U.S. equipment and service companies to be given full access to Pemex, the Federal Energy Commission and other Mexican national enterprises, and its insistence, on the other hand, that it could eliminate neither the federal government's "set-aside" preference for minority enterprises and small businesses nor state preferment of goods produced within state borders.

### *Canada and Mexico Disagree*

Canada had its own bone to pick with Mexico. The Canadians thought they had an understanding with the Mexicans on two key issues: rules of origin and dispute resolution. A rule of origin sets the requirement that an item—say, an automobile—must be produced wholly or largely within the free-trade zone to benefit from newly negotiated preferences. The Canadians believed, perhaps erroneously in this case, that their interests were served by moderate rules of origin to attract investment from outside firms anxious to sell within the Nafta area. In contrast, the Big Three producers of automobiles and the United Automobile Workers lobbied for more-stringent rules of origin to prevent Japanese companies from establishing beachheads in Mexico or Canada where they could assemble vehicles from imported components for shipment to the United States. CFTA's rule of origin for autos, even though calculated differently, was 50 percent; for Nafta the Americans urged at least 65 percent, while the Canadians believed they had Mexican support for holding the line at 60 percent. Without consulting the Canadians, the Mexicans agreed to 65 percent—a move perceived as capitulation in Canada. Ultimately, the parties opted for a 62.5 percent rule of origin for autos and panel trucks.

The Canadians also thought that Mexico shared their opposition to a U.S. proposal on resolving disputes arising under Nafta, one of the most controversial subjects in the negotiations. Washington proposed that if a country disagreed with the decision rendered by a Nafta-established panel in, say, a dumping case, it be allowed to transfer the controversy to another tribunal. Canada strenuously objected on the grounds that such action would frustrate the dispute-resolution mechanism. The Mexicans, who appeared to oppose such unilateral withdrawal, wound up aligning with the Americans. Ultimately, the persistent Canadians gained agreement on a judicial process that satisfied their interests. This episode convinced Canada that Mexico was so anxious to inscribe its name on a document bearing the magic words "FREE TRADE AGREEMENT" that it would make sweeping concessions sought by Washington. In terms of earning the trust of their U.S. and Canadian counterparts, "these [Mexican] chaps just didn't get it," said one firsthand observer. In all fairness to the Mexicans, the United States and Canada were not above reproach. American negotiators, in particular, repeatedly sought direct access to Mexican petroleum reserves for U.S. firms, even after President Bush had declared the subject off-limits.

Occasional contretemps aside, civility permeated the deliberations, and the participants exhibited great respect for each other at the conclusion of the talks. Deputy U.S. Trade Negotiator Charles E. "Chip" Roh Jr., for instance, praised the "good rapport and mounting confidence that developed among the participants as the talks progressed." Continued

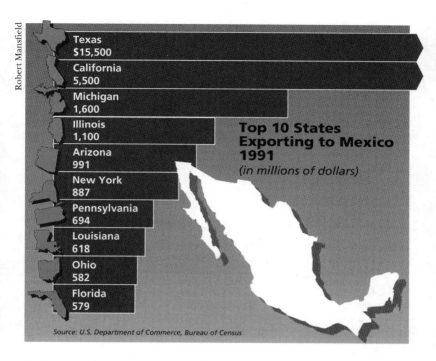

**Top 10 States Exporting to Mexico 1991**
*(in millions of dollars)*

Texas
$15,500

California
5,500

Michigan
1,600

Illinois
1,100

Arizona
991

New York
887

Pennsylvania
694

Louisiana
618

Ohio
582

Florida
579

Source: U.S. Department of Commerce, Bureau of Census

Roh, "The Mexicans were honorable, intelligent, dedicated patriots, who were committed to trade liberalization."

## The Rhythm of Negotiations

The first four months of negotiations concentrated on "clearing away the underbrush," in the words of a key member of the Auto Working Group. That is, the negotiators became acquainted with their counterparts. They also sought to determine the scope of a possible agreement in their areas by swapping detailed information on each nation's sectors, their legal frameworks, their regulatory mechanisms and their trade practices. U.S. and Canadian negotiators in such working groups as energy, government procurement, and subsidies and trade remedies, areas in which the Mexicans postponed concessions until the eleventh hour, dismissed the first six months as a "waste of time" or a "pointless rhetorical exercise." On the average, the working groups met once a month for one to three days. On September 19, 1991, the three countries exchanged tariff offers. Five weeks later, Ambassador Hills joined Serra Puche and Wilson in Zacatecas, Mexico, to review the progress of the working groups. For most working groups, this October 25-28 Third Trilateral Ministerial Oversight session marked the completion of the fact-finding stage of the Nafta talks.

The negotiations then entered the second stage during which delegations to most working groups crystallized their positions in concept papers and exchanged them with each other. In early January 1992, 10 "compositors" from the three countries met at Georgetown University in Washington, D.C., to organize the material from the working groups in a consistent manner to ensure that key words employed in the different drafts conveyed the same meaning and to combine the papers—with a view to narrowing the differences between them. Finally, the draftsmen crafted chapters that conveyed the consensus of the negotiators—with key, unresolved issues highlighted in brackets. In many working groups, bracketed areas consumed more space than points of consensus. In others there was no pretense at integrating negotiating positions, for these "cut-and-paste" texts carried no more than the position of each country, listed one after another. Groups responsible for five controversial subjects (agriculture, energy, textiles, automobiles, trade remedies) failed to produce even chapters with bracketed sections. In the final analysis, the composite texts proved less valuable in promoting an accord than in demonstrating to political leaders in the three nations how far apart negotiators were.

The "bracket-reduction" stage started in early 1992. U.S. negotiators pressed hard for concessions in all areas, including energy, investment and government procurement. Their assertiveness reflected: (1) the greater importance of Nafta to the relatively underdeveloped Mexico where the pact commanded twice the support found in the United States (Mexican pollster Miguel Basañez found that 71 percent of Mexicans, desperate for change after a "lost" decade of economic crisis, favored unrestricted continental trade—twice the support expressed in the United States.); (2) the fact that Mexico's tariffs (on average 10%) were at least twice as high as those of the United States (4%) and Canada (5%); and (3) the likelihood that Congress would reject any accord that failed to contain conspicuous benefits for the United States.

## Looking Out for U.S. Energy Interests

Lending credence to this last point was a continual flow of communications from Capitol Hill urging the negotiators to protect U.S. interests with every breath in their bodies while battering down Mexico's protectionist door. For example, a mid-March 1992 letter from Senator Pete V. Domenici (R-N. Mex.) and six other oil-state senators proposed "guiding principles" for U.S. negotiators on energy matters. Although couched in terms that would apply to North America as a whole, these tenets took aim at Serra Puche's five noes. They included, *inter alia,* permitting private equity participation through risk contracts in oil and gas exploration, allowing market forces to determine hydrocarbon prices, and ensuring direct, nondiscriminatory access to all markets for foreign investment in pipeline construction. Such involvement notwithstanding, the legislators privately told the negotiators: "Look, we know what you're up against with Article 27 [the Mexican constitution's ban on private oil activities], cut the best deal that you can."

Lawmakers regularly spoke out because they were kept abreast of the progress of the talks. The Reagan Administration's tendency to play its cards close to the vest in crafting CFTA had raised hackles on Capitol Hill and in the business community. Ambassador Hills was determined to obviate such criticism of Nafta by submitting updated drafts of the agreement to the Senate Finance Committee, the House Committee on Ways and Means, the Office of Senate Security and Majority Leader Gephardt. Meanwhile, she arranged briefings by USTR officials and negotiators for members of Congress and their staffs, especially those on the 18 House and Senate committees with jurisdiction over trade. In February 1992 the USTR head also led a delegation of 11 members of Congress and 27 private-sector advisers to Mexico City. There they discussed the proposed pact with President Salinas, his key Cabinet secretaries, the Mexican negotiating team and representatives of Mexico's private sector. Despite Herculean efforts in communication, Democrat Gephardt complained about the public's being kept "in the dark." "This secret process, I believe, could seriously undermine the ability of Congress to affirm an agreement at the end of the day," he told Hills in what appeared to be a partisan attack on the Republican Administration. Later, Chairman Rostenkowski contradicted this charge when he lauded USTR for its "relentless" efforts to keep Congress informed.

Communications with the business community occurred through formal and informal channels. Ambassador Hills and her interagency negotiating team convened more than 350 briefings with the 40 congressionally established advisory committees that embrace representatives from industry, labor, consumer and environmental groups, and state and local governments. In addition, individual agencies and negotiators received a steady stream of visits, phone calls, faxes and letters from companies, unions and individuals concerned about one or more facets of the negotiations.

### Principles Underlying Nafta

While generally considered a frustrating, unproductive event by the U.S. team, a Mexican official reported a breakthrough for his side at the February 9–10 meeting of trade ministers in Chantilly, Virginia. For the first time, he said, his country comprehended that Nafta would be based not on horse-trading but on a set of principles—a concept that the United States and Canada had endorsed from the beginning. In other words, greater access for American corn to Mexico would not result from the United States agreeing to import more Mexican-made autos. Rather, the three countries would strive to remove, over time, all tariffs. Four key tenets of a principles-based accord were: (1) complete elimination of all barriers to trade; (2) equal treatment in each country for all goods and services produced in North America; (3) a commitment not to erect additional commercial obstacles between and among the signatories once the pact was signed; and (4) extending to North American partners most-favored-nation treatment accorded a third country. If Mexico agreed to open its oil fields to exploration, development and ownership by Spanish companies, it would have to confer the same access to U.S. and Canadian firms.

At the February 17–21, 1992, plenary session in Dallas, Texas, chief negotiator Katz and his Mexican and Canadian counterparts, Herminio Blanco and John Weekes, made an important advance. Katz strongly emphasized that Mexico's simply making tit-for-tat concessions to the United States and Canada was unacceptable. He stressed, and Blanco acknowledged, that Mexico, as the most protectionist of the three, would have to reduce its barriers by more than its partners if economic integration were to be achieved. Word of this understanding rippled throughout the two floors of the Dallas Trade Mart and energized the activities of the 19 working groups that had convened in a so-called jamboree* negotiating session. Within six weeks, the groups made notable progress on investment, intellectual property, textiles, standards, sanitary practices, customs administration, financial services, banking and surface transportation.

By July the "endgame"* commenced as Ministers Serra Puche and Wilson, Ambassador Hills, chief negotiators Katz, Blanco and Weekes, and team members settled in for marathon sessions at Washington's renowned Watergate Hotel. The rule of thumb is that 90 percent of the work is done on the most controversial subjects in roughly the 10 percent of the entire negotiating period consumed by this stage. Table 1 on page 41 classifies the subjects in terms of relative difficulty in reaching an agreement. During the endgame, working groups with unresolved issues met at length before queuing up to present outstanding questions to the chief negotiators. After listening to the three leads present their differences, Katz, Blanco and Weekes would attempt to devise a solution or, more likely, narrow the controversy. The working groups then returned to the negotiating table until the next impasse sent their leads back to the chief negotiators for assistance. Especially sensitive items—autos, energy, government procurement, etc.—had to be "bumped up" to the trade ministers or to chief executives for resolution. *Ad hoc* one-on-one contacts complemented the formal negotiations. On several occasions, for instance, Serra Puche sought out Alan M. Dunn, U.S. lead of the Trade Remedies Working Group, to restart stalled negotiations in this area.

For millions of tourists who descend on Washington each year, the Watergate complex evokes beguiling images of the 1972 break-in of the Democratic party's sixth-floor headquarters, a scandal that sent 25 Republican operatives to jail and President Richard M. Nixon into forced retirement. After exchanging proposals and counterproposals from dawn to dusk (or later) at the Watergate Hotel, the negotiators had a less romantic sense of the venue. When asked his impressions of the building, Stephen Jacobs, a Commerce official assigned to the Auto Working Group, said: "My most vivid memories are of a sea of bilious green carpets, lousy lighting, 15 of us squeezed into a room, lots of coffee and Coca-Cola, long waits to see the trade negotiators...and yet a spirit of excitement, a sense of making history, particularly among the relatively young U.S. team members."

Another key actor compared the Watergate weeks to boot camp, while Deputy Assistant Secretary of Commerce Ann H. Hughes, U.S. lead for the Auto Working Group, recalled "excruciating boredom" as teams waited for their counterparts to react to offers before meeting with the chief negotiators or trade ministers to address intractable issues. Other participants remembered the ubiquitous bowls of green Perugina mints provided by the hotel. Chip Roh ate so much

## Table 1: Difficulty of Concluding Nafta Chapters

| | |
|---|---|
| **1 (relatively easy)** | tariffs/nontariff barriers; safeguards; land transportation |
| **2 (neither easy nor difficult)** | textiles*; standards; principles for services; telecommunications; intellectual property; dispute settlement |
| **3 (relatively difficult)** | rules of origin; government procurement; energy and petrochemicals; subsidies and trade remedies; financial services; insurance services; agriculture; investment; automobiles |

*Category 2 for Mexico; Category 3 for Canada

junk food during this period that he referred to Perugina candy and potato chips as Nafta's "two basic food groups." Meanwhile, participants in the Trade Remedies Working Group resorted to a liquid diet of Bombay Crystal Gin, Johnny Walker Black Label Scotch and Herradura Tequila to help break logjams.

On a more serious note, two U.S. leads reported that Ambassador Hills was twice prepared to excuse the Canadians from the negotiations during the endgame. One incident involved Canada's tenacious efforts to scrap its "security of supply" obligation under CFTA when Mexico turned thumbs down on a similar provision in Nafta. Security of supply was Canada's controversial commitment to cut oil and gas exports to the United States by no greater a percentage than energy supplies were reduced for its domestic market in the event of a crisis. The other took place when the Canadians balked at a U.S. proposal, backed by Mexico, to permit suspension of panel review and resort to a national court in subsidy and countervailing-duty disputes. According to a ranking U.S. official, the team heads may have confused Hills' forceful negotiating style with a threat to banish the

Canadians. "U.S.-Canadian trade relations," he said, "are like a good marriage in which the spouses occasionally contemplate murder but never divorce."

Ultimately, deals were struck across-the-board, even in such sensitive areas as agriculture, automobiles, government procurement and rules of origin. These accommodations permitted President Bush to proclaim the completion of a draft Nafta accord at an early morning ceremony held in the White House Rose Garden on August 12, just before the Republican party convened its national convention in Houston.

In several controversial subjects, however, the negotiators remained at the bargaining table well after the presidential announcement. The early August text embraced the essence of what the country teams had agreed to, often condensed into several pages. It remained for the working groups and their legal advisers to flesh out the language—and, in some cases, agree upon common definitions of crucial concepts—into full-blown chapters. Although represented to the public as mere fine-tuning or "legal scrubbing," the country representatives continued to wrestle over substantive matters. As one participant expressed it, the "devil was in the detail." Among the issues resolved in this "post-endgame" were devising formulas for phasing out Mexican restrictions on auto imports, clarifying the breadth of the government procurement coverage, and reaffirming a wider opening of oilfield services to U.S. and Canadian companies. With respect to the latter, the Mexicans apparently sought to "claw back,"* or renege on, services they had originally agreed to include in the pact.

During this period, the private sector and labor-advisory groups were also given an opportunity, as required by the U.S. Trade Act of 1988, to review the text and submit reports. Then, on October 7, in what appeared to be a photo opportunity for Republican presidential candidate Bush, the trade ministers of the United States, Mexico and Canada gathered in San Antonio, Texas, to initial the proposed agreement with their chief executives looking on as witnesses.

# The Agreement

Key provisions of the 2,000-page accord for which President Bill Clinton and Mickey Kantor, Ambassador Hills' successor as USTR, will attempt to garner support include:

• **Agriculture:** In recent years, Mexico has imposed import permits on one quarter of all U.S. agricultural goods entering the country, as well as tariffs, ranging from 15 to 20 percent, on vegetable oils, processed meats, tree nuts and other commodities. Nafta converts nontariff barriers to tariffs through a process called tariffication* and phases out, over 15 years, these levies on orange juice, melons, certain vegetables and other perishable items. A special "safeguard" provision will give additional protection to U.S. imports of onions, tomatoes, eggplants, chili peppers, squash and watermelons. The USTR anticipates that annual U.S. agricultural exports to Mexico will rise from $3 billion (1991) to $5 billion (2009)—with meat, livestock and grains accounting for much of the increase.

• **Automobiles:** Mexico has applied tariffs of up to 20 percent and nontariff barriers to virtually prohibit imports of parts and assembled vehicles into the world's fastest growing auto market. Nafta would immediately halve Mexican tariffs and eliminate them over five years for light trucks and over ten years for cars. It further stipulates that these vehicles must contain at least half North American content—rising to 62.5% over eight years—to qualify for duty-free treatment. Chip Roh described the opening of this previously closed economic sector as a "slam-dunk for the United States."

• **Dispute Resolution:** Nafta employs a three-tiered mechanism for resolving most disputes within 10 months: (1) consultation; (2) a Trade Commission composed of the top trade official from each country; and (3) if necessary, a decision made by a binational five-member panel of private-sector experts from the countries involved.

• **Energy:** The accord opens most petrochemicals in Mexico to foreign investment, permits private electricity production, authorizes direct natural gas sales between U.S. and Canadian suppliers and Mexican customers, and allows Pemex to pay "performance" bonuses to successful oil-exploration firms. The agreement still bars foreign ownership of Mexican oil reserves. Observers in the Texas-focused oil patch view the bonus provision as an important step toward Mexico's entering into "risk contracts" in a few years, despite contravening one of Serra Puche's five noes. An important breakthrough lies in greater opportunities for U.S. and Canadian companies to increase sales to Pemex and the Federal Electricity Commission, which have long followed a "buy-Mexico" policy. These two energy monopolies, whose purchases exceed $8 billion annually, must expose 50 percent of their acquisitions to open bidding by North American suppliers during the first year of the accord. The percentage jumps to 70 percent in the fifth year of the pact before attaining almost 100 percent after nine years. Tariffs on oil-field equipment will also be phased out. Trade associations believe that sales of goods and services to Mexico's energy sector will increase by $1 billion or more the first year that Nafta takes effect.

- **Financial Services:** The provisions for financial services constitute a slam-dunk and a three-point shot, to embellish Roh's basketball metaphor on the auto chapter. With one exception, Mexico's $330 billion financial-services market has been closed for more than 50 years to U.S. firms that carry out banking, securities transactions and similar activities. Nafta will eliminate virtually all limitations on establishing Mexican subsidiaries by January 1, 2000. All North Americans involved in joint ventures can increase their ownership of insurance companies to up to 100 percent by 1996. The accord eliminates all equity and market-share restrictions by the year 2000, when this $3.5 billion sector will be completely opened.
- **Government Procurement:** With a handful of exceptions, U.S., Canadian and Mexican firms will have an equal chance to win most of the $18 billion in contracts that the Mexican government now awards, including those let by Pemex and the Federal Electricity Commission. Nafta preserves small-business and minority set-asides in the United States, while establishing a procedure to inform small businesses about Mexican procurement rules and regulations.
- **Intellectual Property:** Nafta provides a higher standard of protection for patents, copyrights, trademarks and trade secrets than any other bilateral or international pact. The three signatories must provide rigorous protection of intellectual-property rights. They are committed to enforcing rights effectively against infringement, both domestically and at the border. As in CFTA, Canada has retained its "cultural exception" to free trade in films, books, recordings and other artistic products. The U.S. International Trade Commission estimates that U.S. holders of intellectual property lost approximately $533 million in Canada and $367 million in Mexico in 1986 alone.
- **Investment:** As is done in GATT, the agreement expands the definition of investment to encompass not only subsidiaries but property owned in one of the Nafta countries by the national(s) of another, as well as services conducted in

that country. The accord grants the same treatment to North American firms as that enjoyed by domestic companies in any of the three signatory nations. Should a host country breach the agreement's investment rules, a Nafta investor has the option of pursuing either the remedies available in the courts of the host nation or monetary damages through binding investor-state arbitration. Such arbitration is the first ever agreed to by two developed countries. U.S. investment in Mexico, which surged from $5.5 billion in 1988 to approximately $16 billion in 1991, should expand even more when Americans gain an even footing with their Mexican counterparts.

• **Standards:** The accord sets as its goal harmonizing health, safety and industrial standards at the most rigorous levels found in any of the three countries. The signatories also agreed that unreasonable standards would not be used to thwart trade.

• **Tariffs:** Nafta provides for the progressive elimination of all tariffs on goods meeting the pact's rule-of-origin criteria. For most items, existing customs duties will either be removed at once or phased out in five or ten equal annual stages. For certain sensitive products, tariffs will be gradually eliminated over a period of up to 15 years.

• **Textiles:** The accord eliminates in six years or less Mexican tariffs (10 to 20 percent) on more than 80 percent of U.S. exports of textiles and apparel. A rigorous rule of origin ensures that Mexico will not be used as an "export platform" for third countries anxious to export to the United States. During the 10-year phase-in period, a special safeguard mechanism will apply to textile products. During that period quotas may be imposed on imports of non-Nafta goods in the event of import surges. There is also a tariff "snapback"* provision to redress surges in imports of Nafta-produced apparel.

• **Transportation:** Most of the goods traded by the United States with its neighbors—nearly 90 percent or $217 billion worth—travel overland. Mexico has impeded such transport by requiring that trucks and buses transfer their cargoes and passengers at the border. Nafta provides open passage roads for railroads (1994), buses (1996) and trucks (1999). This provision should prove lucrative for firms in the United States because of their superior equipment, terminals and warehousing facilities. All of the parties to the agreement will benefit from moving goods faster, less expensively and with fewer problems.

## *Differences between Nafta and CFTA*

Nafta differs from CFTA in several important ways. To begin with, it is much broader, covering such items as intellectual property and land transport that were not addressed in the U.S.-Canadian accord. While CFTA addressed government procurement, it applied only to goods purchased by certain federal entities. Nafta extends to goods, services and construction undertaken by virtually all federal government agencies in the three nations. In addition, unlike CFTA, Nafta provides for the tariffication of import permits and other nontariff barriers to U.S.-Mexican agricultural trade. In so doing, it makes levies on agricultural items more transparent, invests far less discretion in bureaucrats, and ensures that revenues will go to the nation imposing the tariff rather than to the beneficiary of the import permit. Nafta also institutes the first arbitration mechanism for the private sector in any developed nation. Indeed, Nafta's dispute-resolution process is more comprehensive than that found in CFTA. Above all, Nafta— even though freighted with opaque legalisms that make it less "reader friendly" than CFTA—embodies a more modern agreement because of its broad coverage and ambitious removal of barriers to the exchange of goods, services, capital and technology among the signatories. Finally, the Canadians waited for CFTA's formal approval before conferring benefits on the United States. In key sectors such as petrochemicals, the Mexicans have unilaterally implemented Nafta provisions to catch the attention (and dollars) of investors and to emphasize their enthusiasm for trade liberalization.

## Friends and Foes of Nafta

Nafta has enjoyed the backing of the three governments involved as well as major segments of the corporate community. In the United States, the greatest impetus for passage has come from the USA-Nafta Coalition, many of whose leaders belong to the Business Roundtable, occupy the corporate suites of America's major firms, and regularly grace the pages of *The Wall Street Journal.*

Proponents made several arguments on behalf of North American integration. First, Nafta would reinforce certain healthy U.S. economic trends. Since 1988, insisted supporters, exports had powered 70 percent of U.S. growth, and the U.S. trade balance with Mexico had swung from a $5.7 billion deficit in 1987 to a $5.9-billion-plus surplus in 1992. Second, the accord would stimulate trade and investment while creating employment throughout North America. USTR pointed out that exports to Mexico already supported more than 600,000 American jobs—a figure that would exceed 1 million with Nafta's implementation. Third, by raising Mexico's wages and living standard, the accord would diminish pressure for illegal migration across the border. Fourth, it would make U.S. exports more competitive with trading rivals by giving American producers access to cheap labor in Mexico just as the Germans benefit from low wages in Eastern Europe and the Japanese have access to inexpensive manpower in Malaysia, the Philippines, Thailand and other Pacific Rim countries. Fifth, it would spur economic development, institutionalize the local version of perestroika accomplished by de la Madrid and Salinas, and thereby enhance stability in the country with which the United States shares a long boundary. Sixth, Mexico would serve as a bridge to closer U.S. ties with other Latin American countries through the Enterprise for the Americas Initiative, proposed by President Bush on June 27, 1990, which addresses trade, investment and debt. Finally, Mexico's development would expand the size of its middle class and generate more political pressure for pollution control. As David Gergen, editor at large of *U.S. News &*

*World Report,* expressed it, "the developing nations that have joined the world's marketplace are those with the cleanest air and water. Doubters need only compare the skies over Singapore with those over Beijing."

## Opposition Groups

Opponents of Nafta emerged quickly on both sides of the Rio Grande. In Mexico, a collection of intellectuals, journalists, ecologists, union activists and leaders of the nationalist, anti-United States Democratic Revolutionary party and other leftist parties formed the Mexican Action Network on Free Trade (Rmalc). This group argued that Nafta would bankrupt less-efficient firms, exacerbate unemployment in a nation where 1 million young people enter the work force each year, and compromise the nation's highly prized independence. Sergio Aguayo Quezada, a professor at the Colegio de México, warned that the United States might pressure Mexico to forge a military alliance, modify its nationalistic petroleum policy and alter its treatment of foreign investment.

Most assertive on environmental issues were the Grupo de Cien, the Instituto Autónomo de Investigaciones Ecologistas and the Asociación Ecológica de Coyoacán.

Mexican and Canadian critics of the pact encountered strongly pro-Nafta legislatures in their own countries. Spokesmen for Rmalc and environmental groups faced a Mexican Senate composed overwhelmingly of PRI members. Meanwhile, Canadian opponents, many of whom belonged to the Canadian Labour Congress, the Action Canada Network, and Pollution Probe Canada, confronted a parliament dominated by Prime Minister M. Brian Mulroney's Progressive Conservative party. Consequently, these detractors took their case to the United States where legislators seemed more persuadable. Through speeches, news conferences and participation in public forums, they tried to convince U.S. decisionmakers that the accord would exacerbate poverty, civil-rights abuses, environmental degradation and political corruption in Mexico. Canadian Labour Congress and

Action Canada Network representatives, for example, averred that CFTA had wiped out some 500,000 manufacturing jobs in Canada, a contention vigorously rejected by officials in the United States and Canada.

## Constructive-Engagers, Jaguars and Bitter-Enders

Expressing misgivings about Nafta in the United States were a plethora of groups that could be classified loosely as (1) constructive-engagers, (2) jaguars and (3) bitter-enders.

Most active in the first category were the National Wildlife Federation, the Natural Resources Defense Council and the Environmental Defense Fund, with their pragmatic approach shared by such marginal players in the Nafta debate as The Nature Conservancy, Conservation International and the National Audubon Society. The constructive-engagers believed that Nafta negotiations, like the Uruguay Round, would take place and thought it prudent to broaden the dialogue with the Administration rather than castigate its motives and proposals. The 5.3-million-member National Wildlife Federation helped the Bush Administration attain fast-track passage. In backing the procedure, President Jay Hair contended that while "Mr. Bush's position is not all that many environmentalists might want, the ideal should not be the enemy of the good." Central to the position of the National Wildlife Federation and other constructive-engagers is the belief that free-trade agreements that incorporate sound environmental principles can impel "sustainable development." If properly accomplished, such development will not only loft living standards in the Third World but promote ecological progress. Indeed, market-focused incentives might even prove superior to regulations in reducing industrial pollution. The pragmatists continued to press their case within official circles but muted their public criticism after Bush, aiming to stave off a defeat on fast-track, released his May 1991 Action Plan on labor and environmental issues. "The President has pledged to deal effectively with the environmental aspects of a free-trade agreement," asserted Hair.

"So it is fair to take him at his word—and to hold him to it."

Ambassador Hills, long hostile to mixing ecology with trade, reluctantly yielded to pressures exerted by the entire environmental community and appointed several prominent constructive-engagers to trade-policy advisory committees. She insisted, therefore, that Nafta would be the "greenest trade agreement ever negotiated"; yet her appointments were not made until October, well after the talks had begun. Even then, only five environmentalists served on advisory committees compared to some 900 industry representatives. The appointees were Jay Hair, Russell Train (World Wildlife Fund), Peter Berle (National Audubon Society), John H. Adams (National Resources Defense Council), and John Sawhill (The Nature Conservancy). All seemed to take their work seriously except Sawhill who, much to the chagrin of the environmental community, seldom attended meetings.

Constructive-engagers stress three priorities deemed crucial to an ecologically sound Nafta: incentives for better enforcement of Mexico's impressive (but irregularly applied) antipollution laws; a mechanism to attack the killing of dolphins and other environmentally objectionable acts linked to trade; and adequate monies for improving the environment, especially along the U.S.-Mexican border. With respect to the last point, the Environmental Defense Fund, among other groups, lobbied actively when rumors circulated in March 1993 that the Clinton Administration would propose reduced funding for the bilateral border cleanup program.

More militant were practitioners of the jaguar approach, a term applied by Robert F. Housman, an attorney with the Center for International Environmental Law (CIEL), a second-tier player in the Nafta drama. Housman's metaphor captured the popular perception of how jaguars hunt (in fact, these animals hunt alone): "One pursuer races to the head of the pack until he tires and is replaced by another, who, in turn, is succeeded at the lead when he falls back. This strategy wears out the prey." The environmental jaguars see themselves as more idealistic than the Washingtoncentric constructive-engagers who, critics allege, have succumbed to co-optation and "Potomac fever." Symptoms of the latter, according to journalist Mark Dowie, are "a knee-jerk adherence to the legislative fix, an abiding faith in lobbying, and a reliance on ephemeral voting blocs to mitigate social and political problems. Like any addict with enough money to support his or her habit, the reform environmental movement has either denied its problem or explained it away." Constructive-engagers scoff at the charge that a disposition to work through channels either diminishes their assertiveness or betokens their co-optation by the system.

The less-bellicose jaguars demand provisions in the final Nafta package that largely coincide with those championed by the constructive-engagers. First, it should provide for public participation in dispute resolution. Second, increased-trade benefits should be conditioned upon improved enforcement of antipollution laws in Mexico and along the U.S.-Mexican border. And third, there should be adequate funding for cleaning up the environment and building waste-treatment plants and other infrastructure. These organizations favor a concept, first publicized by House Majority Leader Gephardt, to impose a tariff on border transactions. "This is a small price to pay," said Housman, "to purchase the fork with which to eat a free meal."

Some jaguars are more aggressive than others. The tamer ones, according to Housman, are his CIEL, Defenders of Wildlife and the Humane Society of the U.S. The more ferocious are Public Citizen, Greenpeace, Friends of the Earth, and the Sierra Club. These four organizations (along with CIEL and the Humane Society) expressed their concerns in a full-page advertisement in the December 14, 1992, *Washington Post*. Entitled "George Bush and the Secret Side of 'Free' Trade," the piece condemned GATT, the Uruguay Round and Nafta as Orwellian. Specifically, the critics contended that U.S. laws could fall hostage to so-called free-trade commitments. Mexico, for example, had won a GATT ruling that the Marine Mammal Protection Act, designed to

Naranjo
El Universal
Mexico City, Mexico
Cartoonists & Writers Syndicate

protect dolphins caught by tuna boats in the eastern tropical Pacific, was a "barrier to trade." Subsequently, the United States and Mexico negotiated a phase-out of purse-seine fishing for dolphins. It was argued that Mexico, emboldened by GATT's action, would use a free-trade accord to attack other environmental legislation. In promoting the "harmonization" of health and safety practices, Nafta could well harmonize "downward" U.S. standards on asbestos use and the presence of DDT and other poisonous residues in food. "The same fate probably awaits the California state initiative…that requires the labeling of products for carcinogens and toxins," the coalition declared. Faceless bureaucrats meeting in secret sessions, they warned, would usurp environmental policy from elected officials.

In early March 1993, the Sierra Club, Friends of the Earth, Public Citizen and other jaguars dispatched a letter to the

Clinton Administration in which they recommended creating a North American Commission on the Environment with equal representation from the United States, Mexico and Canada. The proposed body would investigate environmental violations as well as pinpoint firms that priced exports cheaply because of inadequate pollution controls at their factories. Although lacking authority to impose penalties, the suggested commission could ask enforcement agencies in the three countries to investigate wrongdoing and apply trade sanctions. The environmental and conservation groups sought a permanent advisory role in trade issues, in the implementing of Nafta and in the forging of future trade accords.

Actions by aggressive jaguars are frequently indistinguishable from those of bitter-enders, composed of consumer and labor organizations, who are totally opposed to Nafta. The bitter-enders complement lobbying on Capitol Hill with challenges to corporations and government agencies. Their opposition takes the form of lawsuits against intransigent regulators, noisy demonstrations, consumer boycotts, shareholder suits and nonviolent direct action against polluters. Most politically potent in this category is the AFL-CIO and several of its constituent unions with large memberships in the Midwest, Northeast or border states: the United Automobile Workers, the International Ladies Garment Workers Union, the International Brotherhood of Electrical Workers, the International Union of Electrical Workers, and the American Federation of State, County and Municipal Employees. The AFL-CIO made opposition to fast-track and a ban on employers hiring permanent replacements for strikers its top legislative priorities for the early 1990s.

Union leaders realized that championing ecological protection had broader appeal than employment-related issues alone. Even though numbers varied widely, most thinktanks, including those receiving union contributions, concluded that Nafta would create more jobs in the United States than it would destroy. This debate placed labor in the unusual position of siding with environmental groups with which it had often crossed swords.

Providing a link between environmentalists and trade unionists were several grass-roots-oriented coalitions. These organizations, which further blurred the distinction between militant jaguars and bitter-enders, also embraced religious, consumer, agricultural and human-rights activists. They were the Ralph Nader-sponsored Citizen Trade Watch; the 50-member Mobilization on Development, Trade, Labor and the Environment, which spearheaded cooperation with Mexican and Canadian foes of the trade pact; and the San Francisco-based Fair Trade Coalition. In addition to espousing "bread-and-butter" issues articulated by the AFL-CIO, these amalgams condemned Nafta as undemocratic, claimed it would vitiate the Clean Air Act of 1990, the Clean Water Act of 1972 and other environmental legislation, and insisted that it would devastate Mexico's natural resources. Bitter-enders also decried torture, electoral fraud and human-rights abuses in Mexico.

Evidence that union leaders were "wearing green" appeared in a union newspaper advertisement warning that fast-track approval would worsen diseases arising from polluted water and food in border towns because of the dearth of sewage treatment and other health precautions. Equally harsh was labor's condemnation of corruption and lax work standards springing from the Confederation of Mexican Workers' coziness with government. "[Confederation of Mexican Workers Secretary-general] Fidel Velázquez is the Al Capone of Mexico's labor relations," warned the spokesman for one U.S. worker-rights group. Above all, unions argued that a free-trade agreement would facilitate the relocation of U.S. factories to Mexico to take advantage of sweatshop conditions, depress wages north of the Rio Grande, and spark unfair competition with domestic producers of footwear, textile, auto and electronic goods.

5

# Evolution of Mexican Lobbying
# in the United States

In light of such Mexico-bashing, Salinas realized that an active, astute presence in the United States was crucial to advancing his nation's interests in general and to obtaining passage of a free-trade agreement in particular. Until recently, however, Mexican diplomats had tiptoed around Washington, D.C., as if they were intruders in the night. While making *pro forma* visits to the State Department and graciously receiving visitors who requested meetings, Mexican envoys seldom traveled the 20 blocks from their former Hispanic-style, mural-adorned embassy on 16th Street to Capitol Hill. Rarely did the ambassador and his staff seek to cultivate key members of Congress and luminaries in the press corps.

At the same time, however, Canada, South Korea, Taiwan, Israel and other middle powers were vigorously attempting to win friends and influence people in Washington with the help of expensive, prestigious public relations, law and lobbying firms. What accounted for this low-key approach pursued by Mexicans as late as the mid-1980s?

To begin with, lobbying meant involvement in the affairs of another country and, as such, flew in the face of Mexico's ballyhooed commitment to nonintervention. A variation on this theme was the Mexican government's antipathy to justifying its policies to anyone, especially to a powerful neighbor with which it traditionally evinced a love/hate relationship. Even more troubling to some Mexicans was the possibility that efforts to influence Washington decisionmakers might open the door to even greater U.S. involvement in Mexico. John Gavin, U.S. ambassador to Mexico from 1981 to 1986, for one, had raised hackles by speaking out on his host's trade, investment, immigration and Central American policies.

Of course, appearing to kowtow to Uncle Sam meant political suicide for the Mexican officials involved. An irony of bilateral relations was that close association with the neighboring country—deemed highly advantageous by U.S. politicians anxious to court ever more numerous Hispanic-American voters—was considered the kiss of death by their Mexican counterparts.

Limited resources and cautious envoys contributed to Mexico's unobtrusiveness in Washington. For instance, Ambassador Jorge Espinosa de los Reyes, who served from 1983 to 1988, graciously complied with requests for interviews but seldom sought meetings with influential Americans. The ambassador, a banker by profession, set the tone for the embassy's inertness. This posture met with approval in the Foreign Relations Ministry where advocacy for Third World causes and anti-United States nationalism thrived before Salinas took office. Also discouraging Mexican lobbying was a fatalistic view that little could be done to prevent the Mexico-bashing that periodically burst forth in the United States.

As recently as 1989, only 6 percent of pro-Mexican lobbying expenditures in the United States was for political and quasi-political purposes compared to 81 percent for tourist promotion. In the same year, the Canadians, who also maintained a low profile until the early 1980s, earmarked almost one third of their lobbying outlays for political and quasi-political objectives and 44 percent for tourism.

The December 1988 inauguration of Salinas ushered in a sea change in Mexican diplomacy vis-à-vis the United States. To begin with, in early 1989 Salinas dispatched Gustavo Petricioli Iturbide as Mexico's ambassador to the U.S., where he served until replaced by Jorge Montaño Martínez four years later. A Yale graduate, former finance secretary and gregarious entertainer, the 61-year-old Petricioli became a familiar figure in official Washington. He did not confine himself to "inside the beltway" contacts. As early as September 1990, Petricioli participated with Representative E. "Kika" de la Garza (D-Tex.), chairman of the House Agriculture Committee, in a West Coast forum on U.S.-Mexican relations that endorsed both Nafta and a "new era" of bilateral cooperation.

The new ambassador selected Walter Astié Burgos, an extremely adroit career diplomat, as his deputy chief of mission. To fill other senior posts, Petricioli went outside the Foreign Relations Ministry to choose competent pragmatists who knew the United States well but exhibited none of the anti-Yankee sentiment associated with the Foreign Relations Ministry. The embassy established a congressional liaison office, first headed by Joaquín González Casanova, a lawyer with extensive experience in the United States. Also, the Press and Public Affairs department was expanded from a director and three secretaries to a director, three attachés and three secretaries. In 1986 the embassy had 50 diplomats and support personnel; between late 1988 and early 1992, the number rose from 65 to 85. And four additional governmental agencies established representation in Washington, raising their number to ten. Not only was the embassy's personnel more specialized, but they were also better prepared, as evidenced by their holding more advanced academic degrees than their predecessors.

A new embassy, opened in late 1989 just three blocks from the White House, epitomized Mexico's diplomatic élan. The $16-million building not only betokened a move toward the center of power, but it also enabled the Mexican government to place most of its agencies under one roof, thus improving coordination and the flow of information.

## All-out Lobbying Efforts

The Ministry of Commerce and Industrial Development, Mexico's lead agency for Nafta negotiations, complemented Ambassador Petricioli's lobbying efforts. Minister Serra Puche and chief trade negotiator Blanco understood that continental economic integration, even though strongly backed by the Bush Administration, would ignite fierce opposition. To win support for the proposed accord, Messrs. Serra and Blanco established an eight-man Nafta office in downtown Washington. Serra's Secofi took advantage of this beachhead to recruit highly respected political insiders adept at swaying legislators and the media. Politically related lobbying expenses surpassed $3.2 million in 1990.

Managing "Team Mexico" was Robert E. Herzstein, a former U.S. undersecretary of commerce, to whom colleagues fondly refer as "Mr. Mexico" and "Mexico Central." Herzstein knew Mexican trade issues inside out, helped win passage of the U.S.-Canada Free Trade Agreement, and is a partner in Shearman & Sterling. His was the only firm responsible for both legal work and lobbying.

The Mexicans and Herzstein recruited prominent allies to help attract support for Nafta. Burson Marsteller, whose clients range from the American Paper Institute to the U.S. Olympic Committee, spearheaded public relations. A key lobbying firm was the Brock Group, whose principal is ex-Senator William E. Brock. Other marquee players included Charls E. Walker Associates Inc., Gold and Liebengood Inc., TKC International Ltd., Public Strategies Washington, Inc., and Manchester Trade Ltd.

Secofi also hired several former Hispanic-American office-holders: Tony Anaya, Abelardo Valdez and Eduardo Hidalgo. In addition to working Capitol Hill, these men attempted to drum up support among Mexican-Americans. In the past, Chicanos had failed to serve as advocates for Mexico in the United States the way that Jews backed Israel and Greek-Americans supported Greece. But Mexican-Americans have begun to play a modest role in bilateral affairs—in part because of their pride in the Salinas administration; in part because of impetus from the Mexican government.

Secofi and the embassy took other steps to activate Mexican-Americans. First, Petricioli convened meetings of Mexico's 40 consuls in the United States, along with his country's attachés for trade and tourism. He urged them to spread the word of the benefits of the free-trade agreement to the Mexican-American communities with which they worked, as well as to local Anglo leaders.

Second, Secofi invited to Washington key Hispanic business and professional leaders. Following briefings by President Bush, Ambassador Hills, Secretary Mosbacher, Ambassador Petricioli and others, members of the group fanned out across Capitol Hill to visit their congressmen. Secofi also sponsored trade missions to Mexico for members of the Hispanic business community. Third, Mexican diplomats disseminated information about Nafta through the Presidential Program for Service to Overseas Mexican Communities. Salinas began this initiative after an October 1989 meeting in Washington with Chicano leaders who sought closer ties with Mexico.

Fourth, following their 1989 meeting with Salinas, leaders of organizations such as the National Council of La Raza, an umbrella group for 134 Hispanic community affiliates, and the League of United Latin American Citizens began to lobby in behalf of Nafta in hopes of gaining favor with the Bush Administration for their own goals. La Raza, for example, sought a ban on guest-workers and increased funding for border infrastructure. Meanwhile, Cuban-American activists, long critical of Mexico's unswerving friendship with the Castro regime, joined the effort "to mend fences and extend a gesture of goodwill." Puerto Rican Governor Rafael Hernández Colón even dispatched a vaguely worded letter to congressional leaders declaiming the "benefits of open markets."

Finally, in July 1992, Nacional Financiera (Nafin), Mexico's development bank, and the Mexican Investment Board announced their readiness to promote joint ventures between Mexicans and Hispanic-Americans. Nafin provides up to one fourth of the risk capital for such projects; the program applies to investments in small businesses in both Mexico and the United States.

## Leading Lobbyist

In the final analysis, Mexico's best lobbyist proved to be Salinas himself. He knew the United States better than any of his predecessors, having earned three advanced degrees from Harvard University. A month before taking office, he met with President-elect Bush in Houston. Their initial good rapport improved as the two chief executives joined forces to wage the free-trade "battle." By early-1993, Salinas had met nine times with his U.S. counterpart, more than any previous Mexican chief executive. Invariably, the presidents used these sessions to promote Nafta.

After an April 1991 bilateral meeting in Houston, Salinas made a whirlwind tour of Ottawa, Boston, Chicago and San Antonio to drum up support for the agreement. On April 12, he became the first Mexican president to address the Texas legislature. "Our economies are certainly different," he argued. "But in their very differences lie sources of exchange and the possibility of creating the comparative advantages that will enable us to compete." Throughout his travels, Salinas emphasized that increased Mexican exports to the United States would create jobs in Mexico and reduce the number of illegal workers who sought to cross the Rio Grande.

Mexico's pro-Nafta public-relations effort bore fruit. Ambassador Petricioli made speeches throughout the country, while Javier Treviño, the embassy's minister for press and public affairs, took advantage of media contacts arranged by Burson Marsteller. In addition to traveling to large cities, Treviño carried Mexico's message to the editorial boards of 40 newspapers in small- and medium-sized cities, many of which were represented by influential members of Congress. Whether swayed by the visitors or not, 13 rust-belt newspapers endorsed Nafta, including *The Plain Dealer* (Cleveland), *The Milwaukee Sentinel* and the *Detroit News and Free Press.* Meanwhile, Dr. Manuel Suárez-Mier, the embassy's astute minister-counselor for economic affairs, logged some 400,000 miles as he made 500 speeches for the agreement in 39 states.

Such outreach initiatives aside, Mexico concentrated its lobbying on Washington. Its heightened activity in the capital was reflected in the statement of a State Department official: "The Mexicans used to be invisible here. Now they're all over the place." A writer for *The Wall Street Journal* went so far as to claim that Mexico had "suddenly upstaged Japan as the foreign government with the most visible lobbying muscle." One Mexican official summarized his government's spurt of activism by saying, "When in Rome do as the Romans do. When in Washington, do as people inside the beltway do."

# 6

# Prospects for the Agreement

Three days before the October 7, 1992, San Antonio meeting at which Nafta was initialed, Democratic presidential nominee Bill Clinton in a speech at North Carolina State University endorsed the accord with the provisos that adequate safeguards be adopted to toughen environmental and worker-safety standards in Mexico and that the President be allowed to establish a commission to monitor the agreement's impact. "There are apparel workers, fruit and vegetable farmers, electronic workers, autoworkers who are at risk not only of short-term dislocation, but of permanent damage if this agreement is not strengthened and improved," he said. Nafta supporters throughout North America heaved a sigh of relief when the Democrat added, "I believe we can address these concerns without renegotiating the basic agreement." Following his victory over Bush, Clinton assumed responsibliity for the continental trade pact. Even before his inauguration, the President-elect met with Salinas and vowed to move as quickly as possible to advance Nafta. In late February, however, when congressional opponents began taking potshots at the accord, Salinas labeled the agreement "a test of the true willingness of the United States to have a positive relationship" with Mexico and the rest of Latin America. "The region as a whole would feel rejected" if lawmakers killed the proposal, he added. Salinas also made an overture to critics of his country's authoritarian regime who sometimes joke that "Democracy exists in Mexico 364 days a year—it's only missing on election day." Specifically, the president pledged to promote fair contests through both a $1-billion initiative to supply all registered voters with photo identity cards and permission for foreign-conducted exit polls to combat vote fraud.

On March 9, USTR Kantor told the Senate Finance Committee that Nafta would have an "enormous positive effect on the U.S. economy and U.S. jobs." Even though some U.S. industries would suffer from the free-trade zone conceived under Bush, Kantor emphasized, "We're going to stick to it." A week later, the Clinton Administration—without reopening the pact itself—began negotiating parallel measures on labor, import surges and the environment to placate senators, representatives and interest groups concerned about these issues. Reportedly, 80 of the 110 freshman members of Congress indicated opposition to the Bush Administration's version of Nafta. Such side agreements will be included in the enabling legislation, which will also embrace the Nafta text. Observers expect the President to send the entire package to Capitol Hill in mid-summer—with the final up-or-down vote held during the last half of 1993, possibly after the August congressional recess. Apart from downright opposition, a factor slowing legislative action on Nafta is the necessity for key committees that must scrutinize the pact to act first on the President's $500-billion program of economic stimulation, tax increases and spending cuts. Predicted big job losses from military base closings announced in mid-March exacerbated congressional worries about the trade deal's impact on unemployment in the United States. At the same time, ex-presidential contender H. Ross Perot weighed in against the free-trade pact.

## Trade Sanctions?

Further complicating the accord's prospects was the insistence by Majority Leader Gephardt and other key Democrats that the North American Commission on the Environment (NACE), a tripartite body created by the pact, should boldly enforce supplemental agreements to improve workplace and environmental conditions throughout the continent. Such action might, for example, take the form of trade sanctions against goods manufactured by Mexican industries that contaminate the air or abuse their workers. Acutely aware of Mexico's sensitivity to any perceived attack on its sovereignty, Kantor insisted that NACE should examine enforcement efforts in each of the three countries with the authority to "review" not "investigate" compliance with local environmental laws. For its part, the Salinas administration has urged "collaborative" discussions to resolve enforcement issues, some of which are real, some political, in its estimation.

Ironically, just as a staunch anti-Communist like President Richard M. Nixon (R) could renew diplomatic relations with China (1972) and a southerner like President Lyndon B. Johnson (D) could obtain passage of the comprehensive Civil Rights Act of 1964, a fully committed President Clinton may have more success than Bush would have had in persuading a Democrat-dominated Congress to approve a trade deal.

Even so, in spring 1993 Washington-watchers gave the accord a 50-50 chance of obtaining congressional approval. Pessimists said that the possible indictment of Rostenkowski for misusing funds would deprive the chief executive of the only pro-Nafta House leader who could prevent Gephardt's disfiguring the agreement. Optimists contended that the former Arkansas governor would eventually go all-out for the initiative because he understood its advantages and because he craved an achievement in foreign policy, perceived as his weak suit. Politicians throughout North America may accelerate or slow integration. Still, the process will continue. This fact is evident in the flows of goods, investments, people, vehicles and communications across the U.S. border with Mexico.

If integration is inevitable, why has President Salinas placed his reputation on the line in backing an initiative that the U.S. Congress could reject? To begin with, Mexican chief executives cannot succeed themselves in office even though rumors abound that Salinas favors amending the constitution after he leaves office to permit reelection after sitting out at least one six-year term. Nafta would strengthen the young chief executive's market-oriented reforms and diminish sharply the possibility that his successor, who will be inaugurated in late 1994, could dismantle them. Approving an agreement would also demonstrate Mexico's maturity and self-confidence with respect to Washington, while enhancing its appeal to foreign and domestic private investors. The accord would be particularly helpful in attracting those U.S. corporations whose officers still regard Mexico as a modern version of the wild West, rife with pistol-packing desperados sporting Pancho Villa mustaches.

In addition, many Far Eastern firms, especially those in Hong Kong anxious to relocate their capital before China reclaims the island, have delayed investing in Mexico until Nafta wins congressional approval. Finally, although continental linkages will take place regardless of what politicians do, a free-trade arrangement would minimize dislocations resulting from an economic merger through phaseouts, snapbacks, a simplified dispute-resolution process and other techniques.

### Enterprise for the Americas Initiative

Even though Mexico was the prime target for the Bush Administration's free-trade initiative in Latin America, the President wished to assure other hemispheric nations that despite Nafta and the end of the cold war, Washington was intently concerned about their fate. He was especially anxious to communicate this interest because in the 1980s most countries of the region had rejected military regimes in favor of civilian governments while adopting market-oriented reforms of the type advanced by Salinas.

When President Bush unveiled the Enterprise for the Americas Initiative he indicated three major thrusts: investment reform, debt reduction and trade liberalization.

The chief executive proposed to improve the posture of Latin American nations in the "fierce" competition for investment capital by helping them "clear away the thicket of bureaucratic barriers" that discourages domestic and foreign entrepreneurs. "In one large Latin city...," he noted, "it takes almost 300 days to cut through the red tape to open a small garment shop." Specifically, he endorsed the formation, within the Inter-American Development Bank, of a $300 million fund to improve the investment climate in nations willing to implement reforms congenial to private enterprise. In 1992 the U.S. Congress contributed $100 million to this authority, which will seek annual matching grants from Europe and Japan.

Bush argued that a favorable investment climate was inextricably bound to debt relief in a region that owed more than $420 billion to public and private financial agencies. The Brady Plan, he said, had curbed commercial bank obligations in Mexico, Costa Rica and Venezuela; still, many countries staggered under the weight of debt held by governments rather than private institutions. He thus proposed "a major new initiative to reduce Latin America and the Caribbean's official debt to the United States for countries that adopt strong economic and investment-reform programs with the support of international institutions." At the centerpiece of this plan lay forgiveness of concessional debt arising from foreign aid or food-for-peace accounts. In addition, Washington was prepared to sell a portion of outstanding commercial loans to facilitate debt-for-equity and debt-for-nature swaps in countries that have embraced such programs. To preserve the "natural wonders of this hemisphere," Bush advocated creating environmental trusts, where interest payments owed on restructured U.S. debt would be paid in local currency and set aside to fund environmental projects in the debtor countries.

In addition, Mr. Bush delineated three steps to promote free trade. To begin with, the United States would pursue deeper tariff cuts in the Uruguay Round on products of particular importance to Latin American and Caribbean states. He also expressed his eagerness to expand Nafta into a free-trade zone stretching from Anchorage to Tierra del Fuego. Individual nations might enter an Americas' free-trade pact. Meanwhile, he urged countries in Central America, the Caribbean and the Southern Cone to tumble trade barriers among themselves as a step toward group membership in such a configuration. Even before contemplating participation in a free-trade accord, nations might negotiate bilateral-framework agreements with the United States to open markets and develop closer commercial ties. "Framework agreements," said Bush, "will enable us to move forward on a step-by-step basis to eliminate counterproductive barriers to trade and toward our ultimate goal of free trade."

### Bush Plan Galvanizes Latin Americans

The Enterprise for the Americas Initiative was sparse on details and even shorter on resources. Still, Latin Americans resonated to the plan; it not only revealed Washington's interest in their economic plight but was mercifully free of the tirades against narcotics and communism that had adorned U.S. rhetoric during the Reagan years. As noted by Peter Hakim of the nongovernmental Inter-American Dialogue, which brings together citizens and recommends policy for the region, the receptivity of hemispheric leaders took various forms:

• In September 1991, Mexico and Chile entered into a free-trade agreement. Earlier in the year, Mexico, Colombia and Venezuela had fixed July 1994 as the target date for creating a free-trade zone among themselves.

• In January 1991, the five Central American nations reinvigorated their common market, proposed extending it to embrace Panama, and forged closer economic ties to Mexico.

- In March 1991, Argentina, Brazil, Paraguay and Uruguay established the Southern Cone Common Market—with a view to establishing a common external tariff and eradicating internal commercial barriers by 1995.
- In July 1991, the 13 states of the Caribbean Community and Common Market introduced a single currency and announced plans to remove all barriers to intramural trade by 1994.
- In May 1991 the Andean Pact countries of Bolivia, Colombia, Peru and Venezuela declared their intention to forge a free-trade zone by January 1992 and impose a single external tariff by 1995. (Ecuador indicated it would eliminate half its tariffs by January 1992 and the other half by June.)

Political crises have impeded several of these initiatives. The impeachment of President Fernando Collor de Mello has dampened enthusiasm for liberalizing Brazil's hugely protected economy and stalled the Southern Cone Common Market's progress. Two military coup attempts in Venezuela and the emphatic unpopularity of President Carlos Andrés Pérez have clouded prospects for an Andean common market. On the brighter side, most countries have begun opening their economies and have preserved civilian regimes. Except in Venezuela, Suriname and Haiti, armies have remained in their barracks—in part, because they were discredited in the 1970s and 1980s; in part, because they do not want to assume responsibility for the inflation, unemployment and debt bedeviling many countries; and, in part, because they fear the ire of a post-cold-war Washington that no longer views the region through an anti-Communist prism. The collapse of Marxist regimes in the former Soviet Union and its erstwhile East European satellites (combined with America's serious domestic problems) has chilled Washington's dispatch of aid to Latin American militaries, once prized as a bulwark against communism. Thirty-one hemispheric nations have entered into 16 framework agreements with the United States, and Chile is ready to begin negotiating its membership in Nafta if and when Congress approves the accord. Argentina may not be far behind.

## U.S.-Mexican Prospects

Whether de jure or de facto, North American integration will have a profound impact on U.S.-Mexican relations. First, a successful trade pact will enhance the standing of Salinas and the firmly entrenched PRI. Their success would come at the expense of the Democratic Revolutionary party, which has excoriated Nafta while it champions a return to a highly protected welfare state. Washington policymakers view the accord as a means to promote stability in a country with which the United States shares a border that is the longest in the world between a developed and a less-developed nation.

Second, the outcome of Nafta will affect the selection of the PRI's next presidential candidate. Should the agreement win approval or appear likely to succeed by the fall of 1993, Salinas may be more inclined to select a successor with the economic know-how required to implement the manifold changes in his nation's economy and legal system necessitated by the accord. Ideally, he would like to choose someone who also possesses the requisite political skills to manage the increased agitation that surrounded recent state elections and that is likely to continue. In three of these contests, the chief executive's determination to minimize bad publicity that could imperil Nafta's approval by the U.S. Congress prompted him to remove the elected governors and call for new elections. The likelihood that the Democratic Revolutionary party will mobilize its backers and engage in confrontational tactics in the mid-1994 presidential contest suggests the wisdom of choosing a candidate who is both economically adroit and politically adept.

Rejection of the accord would produce severe economic problems (capital flight, inflationary pressures, balance-of-payments shortfalls, etc.) that would certainly favor the selection of a skilled economic manager such as Finance and Public Credit Secretary Pedro Aspe. After a year or so of adjusting to the setback, this new leader might undertake unilaterally even more of the concessions made by Mexico in the free-trade parleys to attract the capital desperately needed for Mexico's sustained growth.

Third, as evidenced in Spain, Chile and Portugal, greater stress on individual decisionmaking in the economic sphere generates pressure for expanded participation in political matters. Trade liberalization exposes relatively closed polities to the influence of open societies. The emphasis on market forces also diminishes the number of regulations and, concomitantly, the opportunities for bureaucrats and politicians to exact bribes. Salinas has responded to the forces unleashed by his version of perestroika by reforming the electoral laws, forging parliamentary alliances with the pro-business National Action party, recruiting more candidates who can win elections fairly, eroding his party's corporatist structures, and recognizing opposition victories in several fiercely contested contests. Still, Mexico remains a hierarchical, centralized and authoritarian political system. The persistence of such traits was demonstrated by the president's spurning of intraparty primaries in favor of designating from the capital most gubernatorial candidates in the early 1990s. These characteristics were evidenced again in early 1993 when the governing party raised $25 million each from a group of affluent businessmen to finance its activities. (Reportedly, the PRI returned the contributions because of adverse publicity.) Augmented and more-intensive interactions with their democratic Nafta allies should encourage PRI leaders to modernize their party and to seek more candidates who can win clear-cut victories. This process should diminish complaints by U.S. authorities, human-rights activists and journalists about vote fraud and electoral corruption. It would be naive, however, to expect that either Salinas or his successors will preside over the dismantling of presidential power. This concentrated authority, so inimical to Americans, nurtures coherence, stability and legitimacy in Mexico's 64-year-old regime that is still buffeted by centrifugal forces.

Fourth, Nafta is an extremely attractive agreement for the United States and Canada. Mexico will have greater difficulty reorganizing its economy as required by the sweeping concessions granted to its North American partners. Sectors of the business community have already begun to lament the competition they will face. Luis Rubio, a premier Mexican political scientist, estimates that 80 percent of Mexico's firms—that account for 40 percent of the country's industrial production—have yet to restructure themselves to meet the challenges of integration. As a consequence, the 15 years of implementation will be characterized by legal disputes and diplomatic confrontations as Salinas's successors attempt to interpret narrowly or modify some of the accord's provisions. Mitigating tensions is the likelihood that Nafta will generate much more growth in Mexico than in the United States and Canada.

Fifth, through the trade talks, Mexicans have learned a great deal about the U.S. political system while honing their own lobbying skills. Even though their pro-Nafta lobbying focused on Washington, Mexico has developed a network of supporters that includes Hispanic-American civic, business and professional organizations. These groups could help influence U.S. policy on Nafta-related commercial conflicts, narcotics, law enforcement, immigration and other sensitive subjects that were managed carefully by the Bush and Salinas administrations during the free-trade talks. The rapid growth in the number of Chicanos, especially in the populous Sun Belt and states such as Illinois, makes them increasingly important. For now, however, factors such as leadership conflicts, language barriers, relatively low income and educational levels, and newness to the country will limit the short- to medium-term political impact of Chicanos.

Sixth, immigration may emerge as an evermore prickly bilateral issue as a result of Nafta. Eventually, heightened investment in Mexico will create employment for more of the 1 million people who enter the work force each year. It may be well into the next century, though, before the trade agreement substantially improves the lives of the 40 percent plus of Mexicans who eke out a living at the base of a distended social

No time to waste: Mexican President Carlos Salinas was the first foreign leader to confer with Bill Clinton after the Arkansas governor was elected President. The two are shown here with Vice President-elect Al Gore and Texas Governor Ann Richards in Austin, Texas, January 9, 1993.

pyramid. Salinas's Solidarity program offers hope to some. Still, the Nafta-impelled influx of corn and other cheap grains from the United States and Canada will drive hundreds of thousands, possibly even millions, of campesinos from the land. Many of these uprooted peasants and other displaced workers will emigrate northward in quest of a better life. A continued diaspora of illegal aliens will elicit cries, as foreshadowed in Pat Buchanan's 1992 "America First" platform, from some U.S. and Canadian leaders for more rigorous border management; others may demand that Mexico reduce its birthrate even further. Pressure will mount to decriminalize abortion, a reform favored by a growing number of politically aware Mexican women whose cause may be embraced by their U.S. and Canadian counterparts. Contacts, mutual understanding and bargaining mechanisms arising from the Nafta negotiations will enable the United States and Mexico to resolve some of the difficult problems before they inflame passions on both sides of the border.

Seventh, economic integration will accelerate trilateral contacts between academic, religious, labor, environmental, human-rights and other nongovernmental organizations. Such activities will lead to publicizing real and perceived abuses throughout the continent. In 1990, for example, Roman Catholic bishops from the United States, Mexico and Canada urged debt-relief for Mexico and other Third World countries. They also insisted that any free-trade pact contain safeguards against the exploitation and displacement of workers and farmers unable to protect their interests. A year later, the president of the United Automobile Workers, anxious for Mexican wage rates to climb, lambasted the Mexican government's crackdown on a labor leader who had organized maquiladora workers in Matamoros. Although egregiously corrupt, the union chief garnered praise for obtaining for his members the highest wages in the assembly-plant sector.

## Broadening Trade Ties

Eighth, to diversify its economic relations and defuse charges of unhealthy dependence on the United States, Mexico will pursue closer ties with Europe, the Far East and Latin America. Salinas has even petitioned to join the Organization for Economic Cooperation and Development, whose 24 relatively affluent members seek to expand economic growth, stimulate world trade and coordinate aid to poorer states.

Mexico's opportunities for trading with the European Community may be contingent upon Nafta's success. Even as the accord was being negotiated, European entrepreneurs boosted their investments in Mexico; the country will become even more attractive when exports from its terrain have duty-free access to the United States and Canada if they meet rules of origin. "As much as Mexico needs Europe to counterbalance U.S. influence in the region," says German scholar Wolf

Grabendorff, "Europe needs Mexico to ensure an ongoing presence in the same region."

With respect to Asia, Salinas has reiterated his belief that Mexico is a "Pacific nation." Japan is the country's second-largest trading partner, largely because of the 180,000 barrels per day of oil that Pemex ships to Japanese energy and power companies. Though far behind the United States in total maquiladora investment, Japan is the second most important player in this lucrative sector. Moreover, the Japanese have made $3.7 billion in export credits and investment loans available in recent years. When visiting Japan in mid-1990, Salinas received assurances that the Pacific Economic Cooperation Conference, the economic coordinating body for 14 Asian, Pacific and Western Hemisphere nations, would look favorably on Mexico's membership.

Ninth, a completed Nafta will endow Mexico with a key role in Bush's vaunted Enterprise for the Americas Initiative (destined to be reshaped and renamed by the Clinton Administration), conceived to promote free trade throughout the hemisphere. At the beginning of the 1990s, only 4 percent of Mexico's foreign trade was with Latin America. The integration of Mexico's economy with its northern neighbors will highlight its remarkable economic reforms and make it a showcase for free-trade schemes between North America and Latin American states. As such, Mexico will attain the indisputable position of a middle-level power, a status that has eluded it in the past. Its new bid for regional leadership will be predicated not on diplomatic hostility toward the United States, but on economic cooperation and mutual respect. Even though possessed of both greater knowledge of the United States and more tools with which to manage disputes, future leaders of a growing, Nafta-ensconced Mexico will be more likely than Salinas to publicize their differences with Uncle Sam. Either as a spokesman for Latin America or an interlocutor between the region and Washington, Mexico will have come into its own. Defeat of the free-trade proposal would constitute a slap in the face to

Salinas and be construed by other hemispheric leaders as U.S. indifference to, if not contempt for, the painful reforms that they have promulgated.

Finally, Nafta represents much more than a free-trade zone to important segments of a United States seeking to redefine itself now that communism has collapsed. For many corporate executives, it presents an opportunity to streamline operations to compete against Japan and the European Community. For AFL-CIO leaders, it betokens the hemorrhaging of unionized jobs and the continued erosion of organized labor's political influence. For militant environmentalists, it symbolizes the transfer of decisionmaking from elected officials to panels of indifferent experts. For protectionists on Capitol Hill, it offers a chance to strike a blow for Old Glory. For a newly elected president, it provides both a distraction from domestic issues and a possibility to make his mark in foreign affairs. In the final analysis, Nafta reveals less about U.S.-Mexican relations than it does about this country's post-cold-war struggle to decide whether to step back from foreign entanglements (except on its own terms) or move steadfastly into the global economic arena.

# Glossary of Key Terms Related to Nafta

**claw back:** To withdraw a concession granted during negotiations.

**countervailing duty:** Duty imposed by Country A on Country B's exporter if the latter has received a subsidy from its country. If U.S. firms have been materially injured, a duty is usually imposed to offset the subsidy.

**dumping:** Selling goods in a foreign country at a price below the domestic selling price, after subtracting costs arising from tariffs, transportation and other factors. Also defined as export sales at a price below the cost of production.

**endgame:** The final stage of bargaining when, according to conventional wisdom, 90 percent of intractable issues are resolved in 10 percent of the time allocated to the negotiations.

**fast-track:** An expedited procedure for congressional consideration of a trade bill. Congress must vote within 90 legislative days—no amendments permitted—on a measure considered under fast-track authority.

**General Agreement on Tariffs and Trade (GATT):** A multilateral tariff-negotiating organization, founded in Geneva in 1948, that seeks to liberalize and expand international trade. Its original membership of 23 nations has mushroomed to 108.

**jamboree:** A Nafta negotiating meeting, lasting several days, that brought together the chief negotiators, as well as the 19 working groups, to resolve as many issues as possible.

**snapback:** The right to reimpose a tariff for a limited period in the event of an import surge during the 10 or 15 years when the tariff on the affected product is being phased out.

**table a proposal:** To offer to reduce a tariff, open a sector to competition or advance some other initiative during negotiations.

**tariffication:** The conversion of import permits, quotas and other nontariff barriers to tariffs, as was done in the case of certain agricultural products in the Nafta talks.

**Uruguay Round:** A GATT-sponsored conference, begun in Uruguay in 1986, to negotiate reduced trade barriers in manufactures and agricultural goods and services, as well as the protection of patents, copyrights and other forms of intellectual property.

# Talking It Over

*A Note for Students and Discussion Groups*

This issue of the HEADLINE SERIES, like its predecessors, is published for every serious reader, specialized or not, who takes an interest in the subject. Many of our readers will be in classrooms, seminars or community discussion groups. Particularly with them in mind, we present below some discussion questions—suggested as a starting point only—and references for further reading.

## Discussion Questions

What policy changes has President Salinas championed since he took office in 1988? Why have Mexican politicians traditionally displayed hostility toward the United States? What factors persuaded Salinas to pursue a North American Free Trade Agreement?

What were the arguments for and against granting the Bush Administration fast-track authority? How did President Bush overcome the labor-environmentalist opposition to fast-track?

What are important elements in the Nafta pact? How will the accord be implemented to minimize dislocations in the three countries? How does Nafta compare with the U.S.-Canada Free Trade Agreement?

Who are the major proponents of Nafta? The opponents? What are the most compelling arguments on both sides of the debate? Do all environmental groups agree on Nafta? If not, what are different tendencies within the environmental movement? What additions to Nafta do environmentalists advocate? Leaders of organized labor?

How has Mexico altered its lobbying techniques? Who have been Mexico's chief allies in the quest for a free-trade agreement?

Why might President Clinton be in a better position than President Bush to attain congressional approval of Nafta? What parallel agreements may he conclude to broaden support for the pact on Capitol Hill? If the United States and Mexico are steadily integrating, why did President Salinas invest so much political capital on Nafta?

What is the "Enterprise for the Americas Initiative"? Why did President Bush launch this program? Has the initiative spurred cooperation among Latin American countries? How has the collapse of the Soviet Union altered Washington's policy toward Latin American militaries?

What are the prospects for U.S.-Mexican relations? What impact will Nafta have on Mexico's economy? Will economic liberalization in Mexico alter its centralized, authoritarian political system? If so, how? Will Nafta give rise to more or fewer illegal immigrants from Mexico? How will the approval of Nafta affect Mexico's role in Latin America?

## READING LIST

Castañeda, Jorge, and Heredía, Carlos, "Another Nafta." *World Policy Journal,* Fall/Winter 1992. Mexican academic critics argue that Nafta should be renegotiated to achieve a European Community-style market economy.

*Description of the Proposed: North American Free Trade Agreement.* Governments of Canada, the United Mexican States and the United States of America, August 12, 1992. A 44-page summary of the 2,000-page agreement available from the Office of the U.S. Trade Representative, Winder Bldg., 600 17th St., N.W., Washington, D.C. 20506.

Hakim, Peter, "President Bush's Southern Strategy: The Enterprise for the Americas Initiative." *The Washington Quarterly,* Spring 1992. The plan's origins, provisions and prospects.

Hufbauer, Gary, and Schott, Jeffrey, *NAFTA: An Assessment.* Washington, D.C., Institute for International Economics, 1993. Nafta will have a favorable impact on U.S. and Mexican economies.

"Into the Spotlight: A Survey of Mexico." *The Economist* (London), February 13, 1993. A 22-page analysis of a reborn Mexico and its hope for a bright future in Nafta.

"Mexico." *Current History,* February 1993. Entire issue devoted to Mexico in "the year of Nafta."

Public Citizen, "The Nafta Does Not Measure up on the Environment and Consumer Health and Safety." Washington, D.C., 1992. The Nader organization's critique of the free-trade pact.

Shrybman, Steven, "Trading Away the Environment." *World Policy Journal,* Winter 1991–92. A Canadian environmental lawyer's view of the adverse ecological impact of Nafta, the Uruguay Round and other international trade agreements.

Sierra Club, Washington Office, 408 C St., N.E., Washington, D.C. 20002 (202) 547-1141. Contact for concise statements of the Sierra Club's views on Nafta and trade in general.

U.S. Government, *Report of the Administration on the North American Free Trade Agreement and Actions Taken in Fulfillment of the May 1, 1991 Commitments.* Washington, D.C., Government Printing Office, 1992. The Bush Administration documents in 177 pages how it complied with the labor and environmental commitments that the President made before the fast-track vote.

U.S. International Trade Commission. *The Likely Impact on the United States of a Free Trade Agreement with Mexico.* USITC Publication 2353, February 1991 (USITC Bldg., E St., S.W., Washington, D.C. 20436). Benefits to the United States from a free-trade agreement with Mexico are likely to be small in the near- to medium-term.